BASEBALL IS LIFE

A 9-Step Blueprint for Success in Baseball and Life

DR. MARGARET SMITH
and DUKE DEFRATES

How Mastering Baseball Prepares You to Master Life

Book Design by Margaret H. Smith

Published 2015 by Baseball9Steps

For more information about bulk order special discounts, visit www.Baseball9Steps.com.

Printed in the United States of America
First Edition, March 2015
ISBN–10: 1500472654
ISBN–13: 978-1500472658

ENDORSEMENTS

"I am living proof that the Steps laid out in this book will help lead to success on and off of the baseball field, assuming you buy into the process they set forth. Step #1 carried me through my career in baseball and has continued to carry me in my career in finance. Baseball is a game of failure and can play tricks on your mind, body and spirit on a daily basis. Without having goals to fall back on in times of failure, I would have never made it past the high school level. I was always more physically talented than my peers, but I had a serious issue with self-confidence when I was younger. Through the Steps discussed in this book, I was able to realize my dream of playing professional baseball. The beauty of these Steps is that they also translate to the 'Real World'. The hardest thing an athlete will ever endure is the day that they are no longer able to play the game that they love. The key to my successful transition into the business world was the goal setting that I learned from Duke. I encourage all young players to read this book and to instill these Life Steps into your daily routine. You will be surprised how much better of a player and person you become." – Jim Bullard, Chicago White Sox, Toronto Blue Jays, San Diego Padres, 2001-2006.

"This book is the blueprint for success not only in baseball but in life itself. This book has provided me with the blueprint to teach my players what it takes to become a champion in life and on the baseball field. It has given me the foundation needed to change the culture of the student athletes I am working with today. I can now help motivate my young and inexperienced players to set positive goals to help them grow. This is the foundation towards establishing characteristics to develop a champion's mindset. Thank you for teaching me how to be a champion on the baseball field and in life." –Trevor Woods, High School Baseball Coach, La Puente High School.

"Life will always have setbacks, it's how you deal with them that will determine your fate. I got benched in high school, college, and the big leagues, but each time I was ready when called on, and helped my team win. Duke taught me the importance of a positive attitude. That attitude will lead to successes on the field and later in life when baseball playing has ended. – Mike Lamb, Texas Rangers, Houston Astros, Minnesota Twins, Milwaukee Brewers, Miami Marlins, 2000-2010.

"As a coach or parent, one of the hardest things to teach is how to maintain confidence in a game filled with failure. This books provides the means for keeping proper perspective in baseball and life." – Greg Noble, past President of Upland Foothill Little League.

"This book is not just for baseball players striving for excellence in baseball. This book is for baseball players striving for excellence in life. Dr. Smith and Duke provide a straightforward and insightful framework that allows baseball players to apply the discipline, responsibility, focus and hard work required for success in baseball to success in life. Just as excellence in baseball is not easy, excellence in life is not either. This book leaves no doubt about the connection between success in baseball and success in life, and really captures what it takes for success in both. Reading this book not only took me back to my days of striving for perfect practice, double-headers, and traveling to play in amateur baseball world series, but also reminded me of all the lessons that I learned to apply in pursuit of excellence in life. I wish this book had been available when I was growing up, but I am reassured that it is available now." Steve Fuller, Bishop Amat High School, US Miltary Academy at West Point, MIT Leaders for Global Operations Fellow.

"This book is about what we can control as adults, and about developing good people through baseball. For Duke, the focus was never on winning but developing me into someone who can perform at a high level and weather the storms of adversity. Duke played a huge role in my success as a player and as a man." – Adam Simon, drafted by Pittsburgh Pirates in 2006, played in the minor leagues for four years.

"Duke and I formed a travel baseball team where we taught boys how to be better baseball players, with life lessons thrown in. It became a way of life where players would learn how to become mentally tough and parents would watch their sons make that transition. We learned perspective, pride and discipline. Hats on straight, shirts tucked in, be proud without being a jerk. I watched my son Mike and several others become major league players and some become even more successful in life." – Bob Lamb, Father of Mike Lamb, MLB.

"Danny (Haren)'s success in the big leagues can be traced to his early teen years, a time when a boy needs direction, to be motivated, to gain a greater understanding about personal responsibility, to gain self-confidence, while respecting his fellow teammates and opponents. The life-enhancing skills learned in travel ball with the Dukes served Danny well, as a professional ballplayer, and even more importantly as a husband and father." – Dan Haren Sr., Father of Dan Haren, Cardinals, A's, Diamondbacks, Angels, Nationals, Dodgers, Marlins.

"This book is for all athletes and their parents. Duke brings a unique passion and culture to youth baseball and sports. He coached student athletes, coaches, umpires, and especially parents in the personal values of strong character, accepting accountability, service to others, and being a person you can trust." – Mike Guider, parent and Dukes–Roberto Clemente Humanitarian Award Winner, 2001.

MANTRA

"Baseball isn't just a game. Baseball is Life."

Every moment playing baseball is teaching me
and preparing me for life on and off the field.
Baseball is a beautiful game, a magical game.
It's also a frustrating, at times heart-breaking, game.
If I treat it like a game, it'll just be a game.
Its meaning will be limited to what games are about:
winning and losing, playing to be the hero, no more, no less.
But if I see baseball as more than just a game,
then its meaning expands, and my time spent dedicated
to the game becomes more worthwhile and valuable.
Mastering the game of baseball is really about mastering myself.
Mastering the game of baseball and mastering myself means

Knowing the pure exhiliration of a close win.
Knowing what it means to play in the zone.
Knowing what it means to believe in myself.
Getting frustrated but persevering.
Feeling doubt but not giving up.
Learning what real commitment brings.
Knowing that the most important thing is
how I respond to each moment,
how I move forward, what I do next.

ACKNOWLEDGEMENTS

Thank you to those who supported and encouraged me to write this book, including Gary, Cameron, Duke, and Greg. I also want to thank those who helped pave the way for Cory's good luck in baseball: his dedicated Little League coaches, Bob Mello, Bruce Little, Pete Roebuck, Donn Dirckx, Kasey Jones, his Dukes baseball coaches, Cameron Saylor, John Lee, Mario Acuna, Dante Palacio, Coach Wallace, and Jack Garis and Duke DeFrates, his SGV Arsenal coaches, and his Claremont High School coaches. And I want to acknowledge the supportive baseball community around us including the Frieson, Noble, Santia, Beauvais, Gardner, Opatkiewicz, Hohn, Swift, Corrington, Steinert, Carter, Lopez, Anaya, Cooper, and Hubbs families, whose love of the game and boys have made being part of baseball so positive. Cory has been lucky in many ways with baseball, starting with his fortuitous birthday, left-handedness, being on a string of good teams with good coaches and teammates, finding out about the Dukes a week before tryouts, winning a national championship with the 14U team, being on a high school team with a good new coach, having a great pitching coach, and just happening to be in an area that's crazy about the game. Last, but not least, my special appreciation to Cory, who both chose baseball and was chosen by baseball, our beautiful, calm rock who has blessed our lives in so many ways. – *Margaret Smith.*

As a player, I had the good fortune to play 6 years of youth baseball, 4 years in high school, plus 15 more years of fast pitch softball. It was the best of times. In the baseball world, first I must acknowledge my admiration of Jackie Robinson as an idol and hero. For most of us, there comes a time when we can no longer play the game but we can teach our passion and share the thrill with others. I'd like to recognize Vice Principal Kathy Wiard, coaches Mark Parades, Tom Salter and Matt Hart, from Bishop Amat High School, as most influential and supportive during my tenure there. But most of all, I credit fellow Dukes coach Bob Lamb for my own transition from just winning ways into the players' winning ways. It's not about your score sheet; it's all about the players' futures. And along the way, Jack Garis emerged in the same mold with a fresh perspective of his own. The future of the game is in good hands with the likes of Jack Garis, Trevor Woods, Mike Lamb, Eric Valenzuela, Jim Bullard, and so many others coaching and teaching proper baseball. A special appreciation to my daughter Jonene Baez, husband Tony and grandsons Jacob & Nicholas. Though they may not have chosen baseball as a way of life, it is my hope that these lessons will still help them attain their own life passions and dreams. – *Duke DeFrates.*

DEDICATION

To the boys and men who dedicate themselves to excellence both on and off the field.

To the mothers and fathers who dedicate themselves to raising good men.

ABOUT THE AUTHORS

DR. MARGARET SMITH

Margaret is an author and prosperity coach. She played varsity tennis and track in high school, softball in middle school, was high school valedictorian, has been an avid sports fan and amateur athlete. She received her BA/MA in Economics, summa cum laude, from Yale, and received her PhD in Business Economics from Harvard. After being a professor for a decade at the Claremont Colleges, she began writing books, coaching, doing training workshops on her books. Margaret is married and mother of 4 children. Her second son, Cory Smith, joined the Dukes 14U team in 2013, was on the 14U USA Baseball National West Championship team, and played with the 13U Dukes team that won the 2014 Hardcore Tahoe Championship. After the teams' wins, Margaret and Duke teamed up to write a baseball book combining their experiences and ideas about baseball and life, targeted at 12 to 22 year old players. The idea was to illuminate the bigger meaning of baseball and what boys can get out of the game, no matter how long they play. From the right perspective and mindset, baseball can provide a terrific foundation for a man's whole life, the way he approaches friendships, money, career, relationships. Margaret wanted to write about the core lessons from mastering the game of baseball that could be transferred to life, the type of book she wished she had had as a young person. This book makes the case that time spent playing baseball, 20-30 hours per week even, is okay. But only if you have the right attitude, the right perspective on what you are gaining from the time spent playing the game. By articulating these fundamental principles, everyone can begin to focus on the right things, and make the most of their time being a ball player, supporting a ball player, and coaching a ball player.

DUKE DEFRATES

Duke founded the Dukes Baseball Club in West Covina, California in 1989, and is the namesake of the well-respected Dukes Travel team, which is in its 27th year with four World Series titles. He was named AABC Coach of The Year in 1989. With his colleague, coach Bob Lamb, they developed an early formula for success by breaking the game of baseball down: 1) Catching the Ball, 2) Making the Play, 3) Hitting the Cutoff, 4) Pitchers Throwing Strikes, and 5) Batters Moving the Runners. He committed himself to verbal instruction, being positive with players, executing walk-throughs, then run-throughs, and demonstrating the principles of perfect practice.

He found that by teaching these 5 aspects of the game, he was able to bring great success to the Dukes Baseball system. Duke is a retired Industrial Engineer from McDonnell Douglas (now Boeing), was a teacher and coach at Bishop Amat High School, and coached youth soccer, basketball and baseball prior to that. He grew up in Michigan, played high school basketball, football and baseball. He idolized Jackie Robinson and patterned his game after him. Winning World Series as well as a California Interscholastic Federation Baseball Championship was great, but the most rewarding part of coaching for Duke has been the achievements of numerous former players attaining college baseball scholarships for their academic and athletic excellence, and a dozen playing professional baseball. Duke has always been good at communicating with young men, holding organized practices, teaching winning ways, developing ball players, and watching them go on to succeed at the collegiate and pro levels.

BASEBALL IS LIFE

"Baseball, it is said,
is only a game. True.
And the Grand Canyon
is only a hole in Arizona."
– George F. Will

SPECIAL BASEBALL NUMBERS: 9 & 3

So here's a Baseball book about a **9-Step** Blueprint for Baseball and Life Success, in 3 parts.

9 innings in game
9 players on the field
9 batters in the lineup
90 foot bases
90° angles of diamond
3 outs per inning
3 strikes for an out
3 foot base path
Drop **3** bats
3 hits out of 10 is good

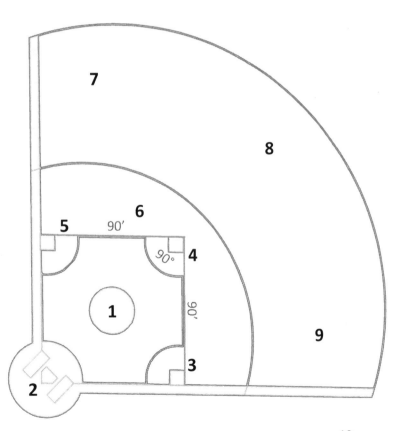

TABLE OF CONTENTS

	AIM	**PREPARE**	**EXECUTE**
OPERATE LIKE A CHAMPION	**1** Set Positive Goals — page 21	**2** Train Intentionally — page 33	**3** Focus on the Process — page 45
LEAD LIKE A CHAMPION	**4** Identify Your Vision — page 63	**5** Live By Your Rules — page 75	**6** Write Your Own Story — page 89
GROW LIKE A CHAMPION	**7** Reach For The Next Level — page 107	**8** Grow Self-Awareness — page 117	**9** Raise Your Game — page 129

PREFACE

Baseball is difficult to play well. And hitting a baseball with a bat may be one of the most difficult things to do, especially when the ball is coming at you at 80 to 90+ mph! There's a lot of room for error. Yet it can feel like a slow game that yields a lot of frustration and little gratification. There are seemingly endless stretches of waiting around with just a few thrilling moments in between. Mistakes and errors are inevitable, and the psychological punishment can be brutal.

THE VALUE OF THIS BOOK

Many books have been written about the game of baseball, about hitting, pitching, techniques, strategies, statistics, the mental side of the game. We don't think we can add value by writing another of those books. Where we do think we can add value is by offering a new perspective on the meaning and purpose of baseball in the context of your whole life. This is not another baseball book about technique, strategy, or statistics. This is a book about how baseball is life, and how baseball is about the process, how baseball can be mastered by following a 9-Step Blueprint for success in baseball and life. The premise of this book is that baseball excellence translates into life excellence. Playing baseball should be less about tournaments, medals and trophies, scholarships, a pro career, and money, and more about how it is helping you to become an excellent human being with a successful and fulfilling life. Of the approximately 115,000 high school seniors playing baseball, only about 1/10 play baseball in college or junior college, and of these, only 1/10 will be drafted into the pros. Approximately 1/6 of these drafted players will make it to the major league after 5 seasons. And of the 200 that do make it to the major league, 40 only play a single season, and only 2

THE BASEBALL FUNNEL

7-10 year old: 3.8 million

11-14 year old: 1.5 million

15-18 year old: 485,000

19-22 year old: 40,000

23-26 year old: 3,500

27-30 year old: 700

31-34 year old: 140

35-38 year old: 30

last 20+ seasons. The average major leaguer plays 5-6 years. Baseball, when you think about it, is an intense funnel, with only one player remaining by age 23 for every thousand 7 year-olds! Why do we mention this attrition rate? To help us all see that at some point, baseball playing comes to an end. For most, it ends at 12. For some, it ends at 18. And for a few, it ends at 22 or 26. Only a handful last past 35. For most, professional baseball-playing is simply not in the cards. That's why it is important to use baseball to prepare for life after baseball.

BASEBALL IS AN INVESTMENT

Playing serious amateur baseball will help you become a champion in life. It helps you to grow: it brings friendships, comraderie, cultivates discipline, focus, teamwork, responsibility, the ability to take direction from others. It is good exercise and motivates you to be physically fit and academically successful so you might get a scholarship or an edge in college applications. Baseball is worth the time and investment, even if you don't get drafted and go pro. When your time with baseball does end, we hope that you will be ready to make a graceful transition as a non-baseball playing adult who is eager to take on the next part of his journey through life, ready to embrace a new career and a new direction. This book aims to help you be the best baseball player that you can be and to prepare you for your transition to life after baseball by recognizing and reaping the lessons to be learned from baseball.

THIS IS YOUR OPPORTUNITY

As a serious amateur baseball player in your teens and twenties, you have an opportunity that others don't have to develop skills, attitudes, and intelligence that you can use your whole life. As a serious ballplayer, you can become better prepared for work, career, business, relationships, and parenting. But this may not be obvious now. You may not realize how baseball is an amazing opportunity to become more skilled, mature, and wiser than others your age. As a serious amateur baseball player, you have the opportunity to develop and test your self-control, self-awareness, confidence, ability to perform under pressure. You have the opportunity to test whether your efforts are paying off. There's no better way to continually develop and test yourself, and push yourself to be better and better in quick cycles.

This is how new businesses are built, how you reach the pinnacle of career success, how battles are won: by identifying better ways to do things, and implementing in short, quick cycles.

A NEW PERSPECTIVE ABOUT YOU AND BASEBALL

Why do you spend 20-30 hours a week practicing and playing serious amateur baseball? Is it just something to do? (We hope not!) Is it for friendships? scholarships? college admissions? playing professionally? We want to offer a new perspective. Rather than focusing on the end-result, what if your time playing baseball was really about the process? What if playing baseball is not a means to an end, but an end in itself? We believe this shift in perspective will raise your level of play today and tomorrow in three important ways:

- You will focus on the right things rather than the wrong things
- You will be more motivated to think, grow, and operate like a champion
- You will have a better approach to baseball, both during practice and game time

A 9-STEP BLUEPRINT FOR SUCCESS

In this book, we offer you a 9-Step Blueprint for baseball success. You will know that you are effectively following this 9-Step Blueprint if you feel energized and motivated everyday to be better and stronger than you were yesterday. If you learn and integrate these 9 Steps into the way you approach baseball, you'll learn a winning approach that will be as effective in your life – as a student, entrepreneur, worker, friend, spouse, and/or parent. In other words, this is a book about being a champion in baseball and a champion in life.

ODE TO BASEBALL

"If there was magic in this world, it happened within sight of the three bases and home plate. All the gems in my world that decorated the walls and floors of dragons' lairs, the sword hilts of privileged princes, and crowns worn by emperors and kings, were nothing compared to the beauty and splendor of the diamond in Wrigley Stadium. It wasn't just a yard with dirt, chalk lines, bases, and a small hill in its center. Wrigley was a field of dreams. Dreams of eternal glory for the men who ran to the outfield, who took their respective bases, and prepared for battle against those who would dare enter their hallowed realm. Dreams for the kids in the stands, all wanting to don a uniform, kiss their moms goodbye, and wield their bats as enchanted weapons destined to knock the cover off the ball. And for the adults who had already selected their lot in life, Wrigley made the dreams of past innocence, lost wonder, and the promise that there was something inherently good still left in the world, come true." – Tee Morris

BASEBALL IS LIFE

Baseball isn't just a game. It's the smell of popcorn drifting in the air, the sight of bugs buzzing near the stadium lights, the roughness of the dirt beneath your cleats. It's the anticipation building in your chest as the anthem plays, the adrenaline rush when your bat cracks against the ball, and the surge of blood when the umpire shouts strike after you pitch. It's a team full of guys backing your every move, a bleacher full of people cheering you on. It's...life.

– Katie McGarry

BASEBALL IS A PRIVILEGE

It takes a lot of resources to play baseball.
The field needs to be manicured properly.
The grass needs to be cut just right.
The dirt needs to be leveled.
The batter's box needs to be clean and even.
The pitching mound needs to be shaped.
The umpires need to be paid.
The equipment costs money.
Bats, gloves, hats, helmets, shirts, pants...
Gas to drive to practice and games.

Just as it's a privilege to be educated,
have fresh air to breathe,
family and friends to love you,
it's a privilege to play baseball.
Be grateful to your parents,
your coaches, your teammates.
Be grateful that you are playing at a high level,
that you are healthy, young and fit.

This alone should make having a
good attitude the most sensible response.

It should make you want to
Operate Like a Champion.

PART 1

OPERATE LIKE A CHAMPION

OPERATE LIKE A CHAMPION

Steps #1,2,3 are about Operating Like A Champion

There are some simple, basic principles associated with Operating Like A Champion that enable a ball player to make success a reality and internalize a winning mentality. Champions know that playing ball is a privilege, so they make the most of their time playing ball. Champions know what they want to achieve, they set up the right structures for themselves, and they execute in a consistent and focused way every time, both in practice and in competition. Champions move persistently toward their goal and refuse to be discouraged. Champions are energized by their goals and motivated to get better and better. Champions take action towards their goal and don't just sit around thinking about them. They have a clear idea of what they want to accomplish, but they are also realistic about what they need to do, and what obstacles stand in the way of success. Champions embrace the daily routine of practice because they know it's the key to their success.

Take time to master Steps #1,2,3

Take the time to master Steps #1,2,3 in Part 1 before moving on to Steps #4,5,6 in Part 2, or Steps #7,8,9 in Part 3. There is really no point in moving on to Parts 2 or 3 if you haven't first internalized the Steps of Part 1. The Steps of Part 1 provide you with the foundation for performing consistently at a high level, like a champion, game after game. Without this foundation, there is no point worrying about a career trajectory or long term development. Another way to say this is, Don't get ahead of yourself. You must be able to operate like a champion with clear goals, discipline, and an ability to focus on the process. If you cannot do this, there is no point in considering a long term career in baseball. Focus on mastering Steps #1,2,3 so that they become second nature for you.

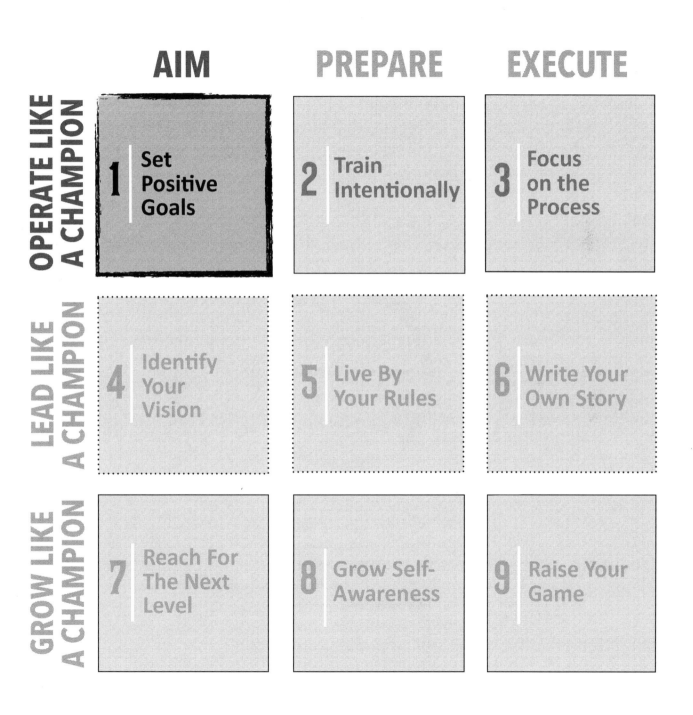

	AIM	**PREPARE**	**EXECUTE**
OPERATE LIKE A CHAMPION	1 Set Positive Goals	2 Train Intentionally	3 Focus on the Process
LEAD LIKE A CHAMPION	4 Identify Your Vision	5 Live By Your Rules	6 Write Your Own Story
GROW LIKE A CHAMPION	7 Reach For The Next Level	8 Grow Self-Awareness	9 Raise Your Game

POSITIVE GOALS
Specific, Realistic Priority Goals to focus on now

CONTROLLABLE RESULTS
All Desired Results within your control

DESIRED RESULTS
All Desired Results (positive and negative, controllable and uncontrollable)

POSSIBLE RESULTS
All Results that could happen to you, desirable and undesirable

BASEBALL–LIFE STEP #1

SET POSITIVE GOALS

WHAT IS A POSITIVE GOAL?

1) a goal that gives you motivation and focus.

2) a goal that is specific, realistic, within your control, and a priority for you right now.

3) a goal that aims for your physical and mental improvement and fosters good habits.

WHY SET POSITIVE GOALS?

1) to have something clear and specific to focus on.

2) to be motivated from within to take the right actions that lead to right outcomes.

3) to learn that you are in the driver's seat and have control of your life.

WITHOUT GOALS AT ALL:

1) You'll be unfocused about how to improve and/or unmotivated to improve.

2) You won't improve and move forward towards your desired results.

3) You won't learn what you are capable of doing if you put your mind to it.

WITH THE WRONG GOALS:

1) You'll focus on things you don't have control over, are unrealistic, or not the right priority.

2) You'll get frustrated at yourself, disappointed, and begin to develop a bad attitude.

3) You'll become de-motivated and stop trying..

HOW TO SET POSITIVE GOALS:

1) Write down all *your* desired goals (goals that are for your benefit, development, growth).

2) Underline only those goals that are actually within your control to achieve.

3) Now circle only the 2-4 underlined goals that are realistic and priorities to focus on now.

BASEBALL–LIFE STEP #1

"One of the best ways to make something happen is to say it will happen." – *H.A. Dorfman*

"Without goals, we bounce around like ships without rudders." – *Don Sutton*

Start where you are. Use what you have. Do what you can. – *Arthur Ashe*

"The journey of a thousand miles begins with a single step." – *Old Chinese Proverb*

"My whole game is attitude. You've got to think positively to achieve the impossible, to be what you expect to be." –*Marcus Allen*

"Strive for perfection, but never expect it." – *John Wooden*

Believe you can and you're halfway there. – *Theodore Roosevelt*

"A man has to have goals - for a day, for a lifetime - and that was mine, to have people say, 'There goes Ted Williams, the greatest hitter who ever lived.' " – *Ted Williams*

BASEBALL-LIFE STEP #1

SET POSITIVE GOALS

FIRST: *Write down all your desired results for this season in the left column and all your undesired results in the right column. Here's an example.*

SECOND: *List a few more desired results you'd like to achieve this season.*

DESIRED RESULTS	UNDESIRED RESULTS
1. Make Varsity	1. JV
2. Don't be a benchwarmer	2. Benchwarmer
3. Bat over .250	3. Bat under .250
4. See the ball well to have a high contact %	4. Don't hit well
5. Pitch over 80 mph	5. Pitch under 80 mph
6. Pitch over 70% strikes	6. Pitch under 70% strikes
7. Throw over 80% first pitch strikes	7. Throw under 80% first pitch strikes
8. Keep pitch count to less than 20/inning	8. High pitch count
9. Maintain self-control through frustration	9. Lose self-control (throwing helmet or bat)
10. Build strength, gain muscles, put on 10 pounds in 6 months	
11. Build core strength	
12. Become faster	
13. To make grades and not get below 2.5 GPA	
14. Find and get onto a good travel ball team	
15. Play with confidence and recover from mistakes quickly	

BASEBALL-LIFE STEP #1

THIRD: *Now focus on the left column. Rephrase "Not" or "Don't" phrases into Positive ones. Circle only the results that are realistic and controllable.*

FOURTH: *For the results that you've circled, modify them (if needed) to make them as specific as possible. Now double-circle 2-4 results that are your <u>highest</u> priorities today. These are your positive goals.*

DESIRED RESULTS
1. Make Varsity
2. ~~Don't be a benchwarmer~~   2. Be in the starting lineup
3. Bat over .250
4. See the ball well to have a high contact %
5. Pitch over 80 mph
6. Pitch over 70% strikes
7. Throw over 80% first pitch strikes
8. Keep pitch count to less than 20/inning
9. Maintain self-control through frustration
10. Build strength, gain muscles, put on 10 pounds in 6 months
11. ~~Build core strength~~
12. ~~Become faster~~
13. ~~To make grades and not get below 2.5 GPA~~
14. Find and get onto a good travel ball team
15. Play with confidence and recover from mistakes quickly

11. Do consistent training to build speed and core strength

13. Get As and Bs in classes

26

BASEBALL-LIFE STEP #1

SET POSITIVE GOALS

FIFTH: *Create a Goals Sheet listing your 2-4 Positive Goals, the 3 action steps, and the time frame/frequency with which you will do your action steps.*

SIXTH: *Hold yourself accountable to doing the action steps, and enlist support. For each goal, rate yourself 1-5 for how well you worked on it this week.*

GOAL #1: Do consistent training to build speed and core strength	**GOAL #2: See the ball well to have a high contact %**
a. Write out all the exercises and post the workout process on the wall where I work out, and look at this list each day before I workout.	a. Repeat a quality repetitive swing by practicing 50 swings per night (10 warm ups, 10 bottom hand, 10 top hand, 10 both hands, 10 "42"s).
b. Do core strengthening exercises 3 times per week, for 3 months.	b. Spend at least 10 minutes per night visualizing seeing the ball, making solid contact, and hitting to a pre-identified location on the field in a high pressure game situation.
c. Do speed building exercises 3 times per week, for 3 months.	c. Practice "focusing and concentrating" process by meditating 10 minutes per day.
GOAL #3: Get As and Bs in classes	**GOAL #4: Play with confidence and recover from mistakes quickly**
a. Get regular sleep to maintain my energy and pay attention during class time.	a. Train with purpose for skills/ muscle memory.
b. Get my homework done everyday.	b. Identify when you have gotten distracted and remind yourself to focus and concentrate on the next play, and let go of mistakes.
c. Stay on top of school work, assignments, study for tests, and ask for help when I need it.	c. Engage in a simple, easy-to-remember process to regain balance quickly.

BASEBALL–LIFE STEP #1

SET POSITIVE GOALS   FOR LIFE SUCCESS

The habit of setting positive goals for yourself as a ball player sets you up well for life. One way this habit can serve you well is in school. If you've really learned how to set positive goals in baseball, it ought to be relatively easy for you to extend this habit to school.

What are your personal school-related goals?
Why is achieving these school goals important to you?
What will you do every day to meet these goals?

SCHOOL SUCCESS	ACTION STEPS
To care to do well in school	• I will list and remember 5 benefits of good grades. • I will establish good communication with my teacher. • I will ask the teacher for help if I don't understand, or ask why I got a bad grade.
To be a disciplined student	• I will listen carefully to instructions during class time. • I will be punctual. I will not be tardy more than twice in a semester. • I will go to sleep at a good time each night, and get up at a good time each morning. • I will pack by backpack each night, to have everything I need for the next day.
To hand in homework on time	• I will keep a planner so I can be clear what needs to be handed in each day. • I will manage my time efficiently and get my homework done in a few hours. • I will not allow myself to get distracted with texting and social media.
To study at least 30 minutes the night before a test	• I will be clear what the test is going to cover, and ask for help if I am not clear. • I will use flashcards and other devices to make sure I know the material.

Practicing the art of setting positive goals not only in baseball, but also in school, and helps to set up this habit as a way to "Do Life." Having positive goals is the first step to being pro-active, motivated, a successful person. Eventually, it'll be natural for you to manage school, money, friendships, career, relationships, and life in the same way.

BASEBALL-LIFE STEP #1

SET POSITIVE GOALS

YOU HAVE MASTERED STEP #1 IF...

1. You are motivated every day to do your action steps to reach your goals.

2. You are eager to achieve your specific goals and then set new ones.

3. Your goals give purpose and meaning to the way you conduct yourself everyday.

4. You would feel disoriented and lost without positive goals to work towards.

5. You feel confident that you can accomplish anything you set your mind to.

6. You naturally set goals in other areas of your life like school, money, career, relationships.

7. You know that you, yourself, are responsible for at least 80% of how your life goes.

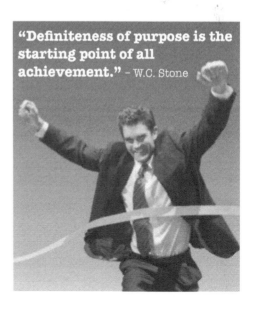

"Definiteness of purpose is the starting point of all achievement." - W.C. Stone

GOAL #1:
PROVIDE A STABLE, ORDERLY HOME

a. Be organized in general, and be punctual in bringing your son to practices and games.

b. Foster good eating habits to ensure that your son eats a nutritious breakfast, lunch, and dinner at regular times.

c. Work on your own personal relationships with people in your home, including your spouse, to maintain general harmony and well-being so your son doesn't get distracted and stressed by marital discord and conflicts.

GOAL #2:
CREATE A STRONG EDUCATIONAL BASE

a. Prioritize education and school work, make sure that studies are given real weight and importance at home; keep tabs on grades through the semester to know how he is doing in school.

b. Provide the best learning environment at home: allow your player to be curious, ask questions, grow, fail, and try again.

c. Encourage regular study times and sleep times to foster good energy. Make sure your son develops a routine around doing homework, studying for tests, and getting good grades.

GOAL #3:
FIND A GOOD TRAVEL TEAM

a. Check out a few travel teams by participating or observing their actual practices.

b. Observe and assess the coach's style and intentions to ensure that their values are aligned with yours, and that they are teaching proper baseball, providing clear instructions, are fair, and building team spirit.

c. Be discerning. Take time to assess whether the fit is good for your ball player, in terms of playing time, learning, maturation, etc. Look for an "Above the Line" coach (p.31) who has your player's best interest in mind.

GOAL #4:
MANAGE YOUR OWN EGO

a. Be patient. Allow your son to play, grow, and fail without putting additional pressure on him. The learning process builds on bumps and falls. Give him room to make adjustments and grow. Be aware of the negative effect of criticism, negativity, pressure.

b. Ask yourself if your behavior is for your child's sake or yours. Be ruthless with the truth. Strive to develop a motivated, confident, mature player and young adult with good attitude and discipline.

c. Contribute to the team by working the snack bar, doing field maintenance, supporting the coach and team, and having a good attitude.

BASEBALL–LIFE STEP #1

SET POSITIVE GOALS

GOAL #1:
DEVELOP FUNDAMENTALS

a. Teach fundamental baseball skills: fielding, throwing, pitching, hitting, base running.

b. Develop strong team chemistry, unite players, develop a balance of composite skills.

c. Instill a passion for the game. Teach self-discipline and teach mental baseball: how to focus, concentrate, relax.

d. Be aware of what each player needs to focus most on, and have a cue word to say to each player to help them perform best in a game.

GOAL #2:
RAISE PLAYER CONFIDENCE

a. When a player makes a mistake, and commits an error, first pick the player up verbally, rather than yelling at him. Remind yourself that yelling will affect their confidence and resilience.

b. Say something positive and move on. Teach them to stay in control, overcome mistakes, and not follow a bad play with another bad play.

c. Discuss the issue privately to address the correction at the next practice. (If you don't address and correct the error and it happens again, then it's not the player's fault.)

GOAL #3:
ALWAYS STAY POSITIVE

a. Don't get too high about the wins; Don't get too low about the losses. Every win and loss is not as important as it seems at the time.

b. Keep your composure because you are the leader: If you let anything bother you, it will bother the players, the parents, and everyone around you.

c. Don't let things get you down. There will be bad calls, difficult people, mistakes. Do not let these things disturb your cool. Remain positive and you will succeed.

GOAL #4:
BE AN "ABOVE THE LINE" COACH

There are 3 types of coaches:

a. _Below The Line_ coaches are coaching for their own egos, for the money and fame, and engage in power plays to keep players under their power.

b. _At The Line_ coaches are coaching for the sake of the boys' learning, development, and winning as a team, but have some of their own ego involved.

c. _Above the Line_ coaches are coaching for the sake of their players, and take their own ego agenda out of the equation. These coaches don't need to engage in power plays or degrade players because players naturally respect them and are motivated.

BASEBALL–LIFE STEP #1

SET POSITIVE GOALS

GOAL #1:

_____

3 action steps   *Accountability*

a.   Did I do this? Y/ N
                                     Rating: 1 2 3 4 5

b.   Did I do this? Y/ N
                                     Rating: 1 2 3 4 5

c.   Did I do this? Y/ N
                                     Rating: 1 2 3 4 5

GOAL #2:

_____

3 action steps   *Accountability*

a.   Did I do this? Y/ N
                                     Rating: 1 2 3 4 5

b.   Did I do this? Y/ N
                                     Rating: 1 2 3 4 5

c.   Did I do this? Y/ N
                                     Rating: 1 2 3 4 5

GOAL #3:

_____

3 action steps   *Accountability*

a.   Did I do this? Y/ N
                                     Rating: 1 2 3 4 5

b.   Did I do this? Y/ N
                                     Rating: 1 2 3 4 5

c.   Did I do this? Y/ N
                                     Rating: 1 2 3 4 5

GOAL #4:

_____

3 action steps   *Accountability*

a.   Did I do this? Y/ N
                                     Rating: 1 2 3 4 5

b.   Did I do this? Y/ N
                                     Rating: 1 2 3 4 5

c.   Did I do this? Y/ N
                                     Rating: 1 2 3 4 5

	AIM	**PREPARE**	**EXECUTE**
OPERATE LIKE A CHAMPION	**1** Set Positive Goals	**2** Train Intentionally	**3** Focus on the Process
LEAD LIKE A CHAMPION	**4** Identify Your Vision	**5** Live By Your Rules	**6** Write Your Own Story
GROW LIKE A CHAMPION	**7** Reach For The Next Level	**8** Grow Self-Awareness	**9** Raise Your Game

BASEBALL-LIFE STEP #2

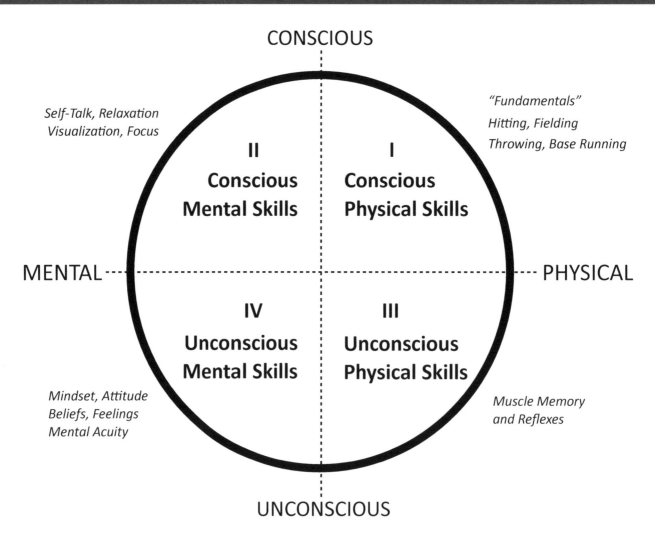

CONSCIOUS

Self-Talk, Relaxation
Visualization, Focus

"Fundamentals"
Hitting, Fielding
Throwing, Base Running

II
Conscious
Mental Skills

I
Conscious
Physical Skills

MENTAL

PHYSICAL

IV
Unconscious
Mental Skills

III
Unconscious
Physical Skills

Mindset, Attitude
Beliefs, Feelings
Mental Acuity

Muscle Memory
and Reflexes

UNCONSCIOUS

Your ability to <u>Train Intentionally</u> in Step #2 is directly related to how effectively you <u>Set Positive Goals</u> in Step #1. You should be able to locate all of your Positive Goals in one of these four training quadrants, all of which cumulatively lead to your growth and development as a player.

BASEBALL-LIFE STEP #2

TRAIN INTENTIONALLY

WHAT DOES "TRAIN INTENTIONALLY" MEAN?

1) To be clear exactly what you need to work on each day, based on a complete, orderly, disciplined strategy and structure that will enhance your performance over time.

2) To have the hunger (that can only come from inside) to be the best, and the commitment to train your body and train your mind, practicing everyday as you intend to play.

3) To choose to take action daily, make consistent progress, focusing on what you can do today, not on things beyond your reach, regrets about the past, or worries about the future.

WHY TRAIN INTENTIONALLY?

1) To take responsibility for reaching your goals and performing at the highest level possible.

2) To maintain the discipline and perseverance to keep at it, even when the going gets tough.

3) To allow the magic to happen: the magic is the confidence that develops as you commit to being the best that you can be, and you learn how self-discipline is the path to excellence.

WHAT ARE THE 4 KEY COMPONENTS OF TRAINING INTENTIONALLY?
I.   Honing your Conscious Physical Skills: Hitting, Fielding, Throwing, Base Running.
II. Honing your Conscious Mental Skills: Relaxation, Visualizationa, Focus, Self-talk, Confidence.
III. Cultivating your Unconscious Physical Response: Muscle Memory, Decision Making, Reflex.
IV. Controlling your Unconscious Mental Disposition: Mindset, Attitude, Thoughts, Feelings.

THE ULTIMATE END OF INTENTIONAL TRAINING:
For your muscles and brain to work together to perform consistently at a high level, when relaxed and also under pressure, where your decisions, reactions, and response are consistently high level and second nature for you.

BASEBALL-LIFE STEP #2

"Excellence is not a singular act, but a habit. You are what you repeatedly do."   *– Aristotle*

"I always practice as I intend to play." *– Jack Nicklaus*

"Baseball is ninety percent mental and the other half is physical."
– Yogi Berra

"Practice, Practice the Right Way. Practice the Right Way Every Day."
– H.A. Dorfman

"I think about baseball when I wake up in the morning. I think about it all day and I dream about it at night. The only time I don't think about it is when I'm playing it." *– Carl Yastrzemski*

"Don't whine, don't complain, don't make excuses." *– John Wooden*

"Discipline is doing things correctly every single time."
– Tony Muser

"Baseball is psychologically the cruelest sport. It really requires psychological resources to play baseball - because you have to learn to live with failure."
– Michael Mandelbaum

BASEBALL–LIFE STEP #2

FIELDING:

When you are practicing fielding, work hard on not only your fielding, but also your throwing accuracy and velocity. For fielding, always start low, stay low, and move your feet to get in front of the ball, reaching for the ball in front of you, and not between your legs, without standing up between throws. Make sure to keep your legs slightly apart, knees bent, butt down, chin up, stay on balance. Don't let yourself get sloppy. Always hustle. Focus on seeing the ball and responding instinctively to field the ball cleanly. The more tired you get, the more important it is to focus on fielding cleanly. Focus on accuracy of catching, fielding, throwing at game speed.

PITCHING:

Make sure to warm up, skip and throw, back up, skip and throw again, unitl you are 70 ft away. Then throw 5 fastballs at about 80% speed from the windup. With control of the strike zone, now throw to the inside corner for a right-handed batter. Be able to throw inside to your "benchmark." Once you have established your strike zone and benchmark, throw 5 breaking pitches, 5 change-ups, and 15 more from the stretch, switching every 5 throws, throwing at 50-60% velocity, paying attention to your mechanics and balance. Your upper and lower body should be in total balance. Stride directly toward the plate, finishing with follow through, square to the plate.

HITTING:

Practice seeing the strike zone as 9 square parts. Box #5 is the middle of the strike zone, and this is where you must be able to make solid contact with the ball when it is thrown there. Know your strengths and weaknesses within the strike zone, and practice hitting the ball in each of these 9 parts to the point where you know you can make good contact. Start by looking for and hitting balls in your strength areas, then gradually make contact in the weaker areas. Practice situational hitting, bunting, hit and run, hit behind the runner, one "get in" from 3rd, swings to opposite field. Do strength and conditioning training on your own.

BASE RUNNING:

Everytime you are on base, train yourself to think about how and when you are going to run depending on where the ball is hit. Practice bringing together your mental focus with base running so that you don't lose even a quarter second step in a base running opportunity. Develop a sixth sense for opportunities to steal or be aggressive. Pay attention to the pitcher's inclinations to throw out runners, get distracted by the runner, the catcher's movements, the first and second basemen's readiness to tag out, etc. Practice speed drills, practice your lead off, slide back, running, sliding, and stealing, as you would in game play.

RELAXATION:

One critical mental skill to cultivate as a baseball player is the capacity to relax. When muscles are contracted, your ability to execute plays at peak performance is compromised. Thus, you must learn to lead your body with your mind, and learn to begin the relaxation process using your mind to direct your body to relax. The key to learning to relax is *practice*! Don't expect to be able to relax at will if you don't practice outside of game time. There are 3 different practice routes you can take, depending on what works best for you: Progressive muscle relaxation, deep breathing, or meditation. (Google these words to learn more how to practice.)

FOCUS:

Another critical mental skill to cultivate as a baseball player is the capacity to focus. Focus requires filtering out all distractions. Distractions are anything that take away your focus in the current moment. Your ability to play well is directly related to being able to focus because things happen so quickly in the game, and you need to be ready to see what's happening, understand the situation, make the right decision, respond effectively. It is critical to practice noticing when you are getting distracted, and develop an easy process to clear away the distraction, and be able to focus for 2 minutes at a time. Practice bringing your focus back to the moment as a deliberate activity.

VISUALIZATION:

Visualization is a powerful mental skill that you can cultivate as a baseball player to help you see what you want to do, before you actually do it. This, however, is not something you should expect to do at will during game time, if you don't practice it outside of game situations. You must practice this skill of visualization, just like any other skill must be *practiced*. Close your eyes, and visualize that it's a bases loaded situation, and the pitcher throws a fast ball right to the #5 spot of the strike zone, and you see it and make solid, powerful contact with the ball, hitting a line drive right through the center. Visualize yourself confident and relaxed, fielding a hard ground ball cleanly. Imagine making a diving catch in the outfield.

SELF-TALK:

Positive self-talk is a mental skill that you can train yourself to do. Positive self-talk is a way to keep yourself upbeat, confident, and optimistic about your circumstances, chances, and opportunities. Use it to counteract any potential negative internal chatter that may be going on in your head. You do it by saying out loud to remind yourself that you are in the driver's seat, that you're in control, that you and only you can make this happen: "I've got this." "No one better than me." "I'm ready." "Stay focused." "Get in the zone." Positive self-talk is a technique to believe In yourself, and counteract any forces that may be bringing you down, or distracting you from what's possible within you.

BASEBALL-LIFE STEP #2

HOW TO TRAIN MUSCLE MEMORY & REFLEXES **TRAIN INTENTIONALLY**

FIELDING:

As a fielder, you want to develop your muscle memory to the point where you bring together your fundamental skill with your your mental concentration. If you get distracted by internal and external conditions, you won't be able to field effectively. As a fielder, you must develop the muscle memory to auto-correct and reset after a mistake or bad call, re-focus, and know exactly what you will do once you field the ball cleanly, where you are going to throw it, depending on what happens, how you might turn a double play, and/or how you will back up other players. This kind of muscle memory depends on being calm, focused, executing well, and resetting for the next play.

PITCHING:

As a pitcher, you want to develop your muscle memory to the point where you combine excellent pitching form with excellent mental concentration and calmness, where you're in the zone. You want to have muscle memory of being totally confident in your capacity to throw a strike anywhere in the strike zone, to control the ball the way you want it to move, outwit the batter and to maintain your form pitch after pitch. This type of muscle memory will enable you to detect when you are "off" and help you to correct what is "off" without having to think too much about the correction.

HITTING:

As a batter, you want to develop your muscle memory for hitting to the point where you bring together your fundamental skill with your mental game. You want to have a muscle memory for hitting from a relaxed, confident, strong stance, where you naturally engage your whole core, thrust your hips through the rotation, keep your head totally still so you can see the ball all the way through, while instinctively making whatever adjustment is needed to hit the oncoming ball solidly while maintaining a level swing. You develop this muscle memory by doing BP the way you intend to play: check your breathing, relax, let go of all thoughts, focus, see the pitcher's release, see the ball, swing and connect.

BATTING PRACTICE:

To train your muscle memory, you should take at least 50 swings a night. Do 10 warm-up swings, 10 one-hand/ bottom-hand swings, 10 one-hand/ top-hand swings, choking up on the bat half way for balance and swing normal through the hitting zone. Do 10 normal swings, starting at 80% and then working up to 100%, with your eye on an imaginary point of contact. Finish with 10 "42" swings. A "42" is how you want to set up when you have 2-strikes on you and you want to put the ball in play: Choke up an inch, get an inch closer to the plate; step an inch closer to the pitcher, and have a two-hand finish. Keep your front-side closed so you can hit an outside pitch.

BASEBALL-LIFE STEP #2

SELF-AWARENESS:

One of the most critical components to training your unconscious thinking is to raise your self-awareness. As self-awareness becomes a more natural way of being, you become more attuned to your mood, energy, and thoughts: Am I hungry, tired, anxious, upset? Or am I upbeat, calm, or relaxed? When you are highly self-aware, you know what makes you anxious, upset, or angry, and you know what calms you down. You know your internal pressures and your external triggers. You know that at certain times, you may be better able to focus, listen, take in feedback, and when you just need to stay cool. You also know how it feels inside when you are feeling "off."

CALMNESS:

You cannot expect to be able to calm down at will if you've never practiced settling your nerves before. This is a learned skill, just as every other skill is. You must practice noticing your anxiety and practice calming yourself down through breathing, focusing, and quieting your mind. Meditation practice is the best way to practice calming down. This practice will teach you 1) how to get to a state of quiet mind, 2) how to maintain a quiet mind for a stretch of time, 3) what it feels like to be truly calm and relaxed, and 4) how to tell the difference between being anxious and calm. This is a way to deliberately train your unconscious mind to be calm and relaxed for you.

SELF-CONTROL:

Another critical aspect of training your unconscious thinking and mental mindset is to practice self-control. This requires a regular practice of disciplining your behaviors so that you do certain things that are good for you, and become part of your regular routine. This practice of discipline builds the capacity for self-control, which is the capacity to choose which behaviors you will engage in and which you will not engage in. For example, you practice self-control when you choose to do your stretching every day, when you sleep at a regular time, eat a healthy diet. You also practice self-control when you do your homework, hand in assignments on time. All these aspects of self-control can be learned and practiced.

WINNING ATTITUDE:

Another aspect of training your unconscious thinking is practicing controlling your attitude. Learning to maintain a winning attitude is about thinking and behaving for the win, whether you are losing or winning. If you are losing, or down in the count, a winning attitude carries with it the unshakeable belief that it is possible to come from behind to victory. If you are winning, a winning attitude does not let up but focuses intently to ensure the win. A winning attitude is an attitude that is positive and determined. You can practice cultivating a winning attitude through a combination of self-awareness and self-talk. Notice if you get pessimistic and negative and direct yourself to correct this through self-talk.

BASEBALL—LIFE STEP #2

YOU HAVE MASTERED STEP #2 IF...

1. You are a person not just of words, but of action.

2. You train your body and your mind, taking both to be equally important to your success.

3. You are self-disciplined about the way you train everyday.

4. Your commitment and dedication to your training is at the top 10% of your class.

5. You feel incomplete and bad if you haven't done your training for the day.

6. You are aware of and in control of your feelings, thoughts, words, and actions.

7. Your work ethic earns the respect of those around you.

"Winning isn't everything, but wanting to win is."
— Vince Lombardi

BASEBALL-LIFE STEP #2

PATIENCE: Practice patience with your son and your family, knowing that no one is perfect, and it takes time to grow into the person that they can become.

RULES: Make sure you are clear what you expect from your son, in terms of school work, chores, and attitude, and hold him accountable for living up to your rules. This will help you to create a strong home base, from which he can flourish.

MENTAL

Practice areas
Patience
Gratitude
Presence

PHYSICAL

Practice areas
Setting Rules
Organization
Self-Control

GRATITUDE: Practice appreciating your son, your family, yourself. This will help you to be a pleasant, stabilizing force in your family.

ORGANIZATION: Practice being organized about meals, money, scheduling, and time. It will help both you and your son have the order, structure, nutrition, resources, and support to be successful in life.

PRESENCE: Practice being a calm, supportive presence for your son and family. This means being able to be there for them, through thick and thin, without criticizing, yelling, or falling apart.

SELF-CONTROL: Learn to control your words and emotions, so that you can be a pleasant, positive parent, rather than a grumpy, negative, criticizing parent. Remember that your son needs your patience and sensitivity, as much as he needs your advice and tips.

BASEBALL-LIFE STEP #2

TRAIN INTENTIONALLY

COMPOSURE: Practice keeping your cool, both on and off the field, as a way to train yourself to keep your cool towards players, opponents, and umpires.

POSITIVITY: Practice seeing the positive side of things, as a way to appreciate your players, your team, yourself, and the progress that you are making with them. You will earn players' respect and motivate them to try their best.

RULES: Make sure you establish clear rules and boundaries for your players and youself, so that everyone knows what you expect and why. It is for the sake of fairness, clarity, discipline, and integrity.

ORGANIZATION: Practice being organized and efficient in the way you run practice and games, so that each player, and the overall team, can improve the most possible from game to game.

MENTAL

Practice areas
Composure
Positivity
Empathy

PHYSICAL

Practice areas
Setting Rules
Organization
Praise

EMPATHY: Practice putting yourself in another person's shoes. Ask yourself what you would feel if you were them. This will help you to relate to people more effectively, allowing you to mentor and teach more effectively.

PRAISE: Say something "positive" to every player, both privately and in front of the whole team. Every player has a strength. Say it to him. Let him know that he does something special.

BASEBALL–LIFE STEP #2

You cannot <u>Train Intentionally</u> without a **ROUTINE** that establishes regularity, consistency, and momentum. Without regularity, you will do different parts of your training in fits and starts, which means that your learning curve will be slow and flat. Without consistency, you will not be able to gradully increase the difficulty and intensity of your workouts to raise your strength, speed, coordination, and everything else that takes time to build up. Without momentum, you will not be able to persevere through the difficult times. This *sample worksheet* gives you a way to develop a training routine that works with your schedule, so that you will stick to it everyday.

Times	Monday	Tuesday	Wednesday	Thursday	Friday	Saturday	Sunday
6 - 6:30 am	**strength**	**strength**	**speed**	**weights**	**speed**	sleeping	sleeping
6:30-12 pm	SCHOOL	SCHOOL	SCHOOL	SCHOOL	SCHOOL	TEAM GAME	sleeping
12-2:30 pm	SCHOOL	SCHOOL	SCHOOL	SCHOOL	SCHOOL	**stretching**	**speed/ weights**
2:30-5:30	team practice	team practice	team practice	team practice	team practice	homework	homework
5:30-6:30	dinner	dinner	dinner	dinner	dinner	dinner	dinner
6:30-9:30	homework	homework	homework	homework	friends	free time	homework
9:30-10:00	**abs**	**abs**	**stretching**	**abs**	**stretching**	**abs**	**abs**
10:00 pm	lights out	lights out	lights out	lights out	lights out	lights out	lights out

	AIM	**PREPARE**	**EXECUTE**
OPERATE LIKE A CHAMPION	**1** Set Positive Goals	**2** Train Intentionally	**3** Focus on the Process
LEAD LIKE A CHAMPION	**4** Identify Your Vision	**5** Live By Your Rules	**6** Write Your Own Story
GROW LIKE A CHAMPION	**7** Reach For The Next Level	**8** Grow Self-Awareness	**9** Raise Your Game

A. FOCUS
Filter out all distractions, begin mental preparation, assess situation, get clear on what you will do, visualize, do directive self-talk.

B. RELAX
Use your mind to control your body. Do controlled breathing to calm your heart rate, blood pressure, relax, and get in the zone.

FOCUS ON THE PROCESS

D. EXECUTE
Intentionally execute the action exactly as you have practiced (mind over matter) based on your intentional training of practicing as you intend to play.

C. LOCK IN
Quiet your mind, Concentrate, and Lock In to your Focal Point.

Your ability to Focus on the Process in Step #3 is directly related to how you Train Intentionally in Step #2. Focusing on the Process requires conscious and unconscious mental and physical skills. With solid fundamental skills anchored in you, you can trust that you have the skills to react well.

BASEBALL–LIFE STEP #3

WHAT IS A PROCESS?
1) A repeatable sequence of thoughts and actions, like a level swing through the strike zone.
2) The best sequence of steps to ensure the most consistent, high level execution.
3) A way to master a particular situation that involves all aspects of your intentional training.

WHAT DOES "FOCUS ON THE PROCESS" MEAN?
1) It means to do exactly what needs to be done in this moment, free of all distractions.
2) It means to stay in the moment, and not get ahead of yourself thinking about results.
3) It means to execute exactly as you've done in practice, at a high level, with consistency.

WHY IS IT CRITICAL TO "FOCUS ON THE PROCESS"?
1) To apply the greatest focus on the activity at hand, not allowing your mind to wander.
2) To play with utmost confidence, a winning mindset, and perform like a champion.
3) To finish and bring all the hard work and intentional training to fruition.

WHAT IS THE 4-PART SEQUENCE TO "FOCUS ON THE PROCESS"?
A. Focus: Filter out distractions, mentally prepare, assess, get clear, visualize, self-talk.
B. Relax: Do controlled breathing to calm your heart rate, blood pressure, get in the zone.
C. Lock In: Quiet your mind, concentrate, and lock in on your focal point.
D. Execute: Intentionally execute the action exactly as you have practiced.

WHAT MAKES FOCUSING ON THE PROCESS SO DIFFICULT?
1) Your monkey mind wants to be in control, and does not want to let you to be in control.
2) It requires great mental discipline to only focus on what's controllable, not uncontrollable.
3) It takes time to cultivate the mental discipline needed to overcome monkey mind.

BASEBALL-LIFE STEP #3

Check all that have applied to you

INTERNAL PRESSURE:
- [ ] "I've got to get a hit."
- [ ] "I have to strike this guy out."
- [ ] "We've got to win this game."
- [ ] "I want to show the coach I can hit."
- [ ] "I'm going to prove I deserve a spot."
- [ ] "I don't want to make a mistake."

COMPLAINT:
- [ ] "This field sucks."
- [ ] "How can anyone pitch on this mound?"
- [ ] "I can't believed he dropped the ball."
- [ ] "I can't believe the ump called that a strike!"
- [ ] "I just don't feel like being here today."
- [ ] "It's so hot."
- [ ] "My dad is putting a lot of pressure on me."
- [ ] "Why aren't I in the starting lineup?"
- [ ] "I don't want to be playing in the outfield."

BAD ATTITUDE:
- [ ] "It's not my day."
- [ ] "I hope I don't strike out."
- [ ] "I don't feel up to it today."
- [ ] "This pitcher is going to strike me out."
- [ ] "This hitter can hit anything I throw him"
- [ ] "I know we're going to lose"
- [ ] "This isn't an important game."
- [ ] "There's no one important watching today."

OVER-CONFIDENCE:
- [ ] "No one can strike me out. I'm on fire today."
- [ ] "I'm going to pitch a no-hitter today."
- [ ] "I want to keep my record as the best hitter on the team."

BASEBALL-LIFE STEP #3

FOCUS ON THE PROCESS

OUTSIDE PRESSURE:
from coaches, teammates, parents, outsiders, media

AUDIENCE / CROWD NOISE:
Jeering, commenting, heckling

INNER PRESSURE:
The pressure you put on yourself to succeed, or not make a mistake

POOR FIELD CONDITIONS:
Rain, heat, wind, sun, bumps

NEGATIVITY & INNER CHATTER:
Self-talk that is negative, causing worry, anxiety, lack of confidence

EXTREME EMOTIONS:
Anger, frustration, upset, resentment, disappointment

DISTRACTIONS

I'm not good enough

POOR PHYSICAL STATE:
Tired, fatigued, hungry, dehydrated, in pain

UMPIRE CALLS:
Ump makes a bad call

TEAMMATE ERROR:
Someone on your team makes a bad error

BASEBALL—LIFE STEP #3

"If you do it because you love it, and you don't care about whether you're seen or not, paid or not, then all that stuff will come. But enjoy the process! If you start doing things for the sake of rewards, then it's going to catch up to you. The other guys not chasing money are going to outdo you in the end, because real grit comes from loving the process." – *Rodney Mullen*

"Think! How the heck are you gonna think and hit at the same time? – *Yogi Berra*

"In baseball, my theory is to strive for consistency, not to worry about the numbers. If you dwell on statistics, you get shortsighted. If you aim for consistency, the numbers will be there at the end." – *Tom Seaver*

"I am the same in every situation. Whether it's an at-bat at spring training or a World Series game, I think the same and I feel the same. I will be the same person if I get a hit or if I make an out. I'm good when the chips are down, because a lot of players tighten up and aren't as good. I'm just me."– *Al Oliver*

"Big things are accomplished only through the perfection of minor details."– *John Wooden*

"Don't let any game be 'too big.' Take it like any other game. Don't let yourself over think. Stick with your normal routines."

A. FOCUS

It's impossible to focus if you're confused or distracted.

1. Begin by assessing the game situation. Where are the runners? How many outs? Who might steal? Gaps? Patterns? Opportunities? Weaknesses, speed, tendencies?
2. Decide how you want to respond and adapt to this current moment. Be crystal clear about your plan, so you have zero confusion or uncertainty about what you are going to do. (e.g. Hit the ball into the gap, take an extra lead off step, throw a first pitch strike, etc.). Say it out loud to yourself.
3. Filter out all distractions (see p.48-49). Don't overthink. Amateur Mind is bothered by distractions, that has not learned to filter them out. Champion Mind has developed the mental discipline to stop monkey mind chatter, filters out distractions, doesn't overthink.
4. Use Self-Talk to cue yourself to be positive, focus, ready.
5. Visualize yourself executing the move flawlessly. See it in your mind's eye.

B. RELAX

It's impossible to relax if you're not in the moment.

To be in the zone means to be calm and empty of mind, and relaxed and confident in body, not holding onto anything from the past or anticipating the future. Any muscle tension, even ever so slight, will lead you to underperform your natural ability.

1. Stretch your arms out and loosen your body for 30 seconds.
2. Squinch your face, then relax muscles in your face (30 sec).
3. Rotate your neck twice to the right, and twice to the left.
4. Roll your shoulders forward twice and backwards twice.
5. Breathe in through your nose and hold it for 2 seconds.
6. Strongly exhale through your mouth and as you exhale, let go of all thoughts in your mind.
7. Breathe in through your nose and hold it for 2 seconds.
8. Strongly exhale through your mouth and as you exhale, let go of all emotions in your heart.
9. Breathe in through your nose and hold it for 2 seconds.
10. Strongly exhale through your mouth and as you exhale, let go of all tensions in your body.

D. EXECUTION

Execution requires Focus, Relaxation, Lock-In, Follow-Through:

This is the part where you do exactly what you've practiced.

1. Allow your muscle memory and instinct to help you execute flawlessly and consistently. Trust your process.
2. If you have done the 3 preceding steps perfectly, then you have done exactly what you have asked of yourself. If you make an error in execution, you must let it go and move on to the next moment. Focus on the process. Continue to go through exactly the same sequence of steps outlined here as you've practiced during training, and have done in the game.
3. You may make mental adjustments or physical adjustments as appropriate to the game situation (pitch count, runners on base, etc), but do not change the way you prepare and focus on your process.
4. Have faith that you are prepared and know what to do, and can and will do in the game.

C. LOCK IN

Locking-in requires a period of concentration of about 20 sec:

We can say that the lock-in process is comprised of 2 parts: loose focus and strong focus. The lock-in process triggers a sequence of moves that leads to the complete and successful execution of the kinetic chain of events

1. For pitching, the pitcher should lock-in to the catcher's glove as a way to cue himself as he moves into his windup/stretch.
2. For hitting, the batter must be able to hold loose focus on the pitcher until the pitcher goes into the windup or stretch. This can last anywhere from 2 seconds to 20 seconds. Once the pitcher goes into his windup, the batter must be able to lock-in to the pitcher's hand and ball release with strong focus for another 2 to 15 seconds of concentration.
3. Because our brains can only hold strong focus for a few seconds at a time, it is important to develop the capacity to hold strong focus. Know your limits and toggle from loose focus to strong focus at the right time before the action.
4. Strong focus triggers your instinctual mental and physical reflex to react as you've practiced hundreds of times before.

BASEBALL-LIFE STEP #3

A. FOCUS

1. As a fielder, begin focusing when the batter enters the batter's box.
2. Check where the runners are, who is likely to steal, pay attention to their lead offs, their body language, and their likely running choice.
3. Anticipate how to make the play for different scenarios.
4. Visualize making the play.
5. Charge balls on the ground, hustle for fly balls.
6. Tell yourself to stay focused and let go of bad plays, yours or your teammates'.
7. Communicate the plan to teammates.

B. RELAX

1. You want to maintain confident, strong body language.
2. Check your breathing and heart rate, mindset and attitude.
3. Breathe, relax, and gather yourself. Follow the relaxation process on page 51.
4. Want the ball to be hit to you!
5. Trust that you will make the play, and make a good throw.

D. EXECUTION

1. Once the ball is hit, engage good footwork, moving towards the ball, or your base, or the cutoff position, depending on whether you anticipate fielding the ball.
2. Always hustle, charge ground balls, run towards fly balls, communicate with your teammates, and hustle for bunts and fouls.
3. Catch the ball and make the play.
4. Follow your throw with your eyes.
5. Recover focus for the next batter or at bat.

C. LOCK IN

1. Maintain loose focus on the batter and runners when the batter is in the batter's box.
2. When the batter begins to engage, and steps into the hit, engage your strong focus on the batter and bat.
3. Read the batter and the ball.
4. Anticipate how the ball is going to come off the bat, where it is going, what you are going to do, and how you are going to back your teammates up.

BASEBALL-LIFE STEP #3

FOCUS ON THE PROCESS

A. FOCUS

1. Throw one pitch at a time. Keep your cool. Don't let past success or failure affect this pitch. Start with a clean slate for each pitch. Focus on your process, and keep your tempo.
2. Decide where you want to pitch it and how.
3. Clear your mind. Remind yourself about shifting your weight back, then forward, glove positioning, balance, follow through.
4. Tell yourself to stay focused and intense.
5. Visualize yourself throwing exactly the kind of pitch you intend to throw.

B. RELAX

1. Pitching is all about disrupting the hitter's timing. You must maintain your calm and confidence in order to execute exactly as you intend to.
2. Therefore, it is critical to calm your body and mind. Check your breathing and heart rate. Check your mindset. It's easy to get frustrated but you cannot allow this to happen.
3. Follow the steps on page 51 to relax yourself.

D. EXECUTION

1. How effectively you pitch the ball depends on good body mechanics, a good tempo, and effective recovery and resetting for this pitch right now.
2. Good body mechanics depends on how well you shift your weight from back to front, maintain your glove position at the right height, push off, step straight, stride forward, accelerate, balance on your landing leg, decelerate, balance in the delivery and finish.
3. Maintaining good body mechanics and mental focus pitch after pitch demonstrates true focus on the process, discipline, and mastery.

C. LOCK IN

1. Keep a loose focus on the catcher and runners until you are ready to pitch the ball.
2. If you notice that you are distracted, are not focusing on your process, step off the mound and reset yourself.
3. Once you are ready to pitch, lock in to the catcher's glove, commit to your pitch, and move into your windup.

BASEBALL-LIFE STEP #3

A. FOCUS

1. For your at bat, begin to focus when you enter the on-deck circle. Assess the game situation, where the runners are, gaps in the infield, pitcher's weaknesses/tendencies.
2. Decide where and how you want to hit the ball, and what kind of pitch you are going to go for. (Expect a fast ball down the middle, and make adjustments as needed).
3. Clear your mind. Tell yourself to see the ball, keep your head still, balance, focus on process.
4. Visualize yourself hitting a particular type of pitch (e.g. a fast ball down the middle, line drive straight through the gap between 1 & 2.)

B. RELAX

1. You want to enter the batter's box relaxed, so begin your relaxation process after you've completed your focusing process, while you are in the on-deck circle. Check whether you are anxious. Check your mental attitude. How is your breathing, heart rate? Are you calm?
2. In the on-deck circle, gather yourself, go through the relaxation process on page 51.
3. Practice till you know what it means to enter the batter's box totally calm and confident, and hold yourself accountable to master this.

D. EXECUTION

1. How well you keep your head still, see the ball, track the ball the entire length of its pathway, and anticipate the movement of the ball will determine how well you make contact
2. As you see the pitcher begin to pitch, bring your front leg up, track the ball, step, swing.
3. Your swing, timing, motion will change based on speed and pitch location; there will be more pelvis rotation and open angle on inside pitches. The upper trunk will rotate faster, and there will be different shoulder and elbow movement for high inside pitches.

C. LOCK IN

1. Level head, eyes pointed at pitcher with a loose focus. Don't let your mind wander.
2. If you notice that you've been disrupted in your process, and need to reset, step out of the batter's box until you are ready. Then step back in ready to maintain a loose focus again.
3. Once you see that the pitcher is moving into his windup/stretch, begin to hold a strong focus on the pitcher. If the pitcher takes too long, reset, and re-focus.
4. See the ball's release clearly. Prepare to move through your hitting process with precision and consistency.

BASEBALL-LIFE STEP #3

YOU HAVE MASTERED STEP #3 IF...

1. You filter out internal and external distractions to focus on the moment at hand.

2. You don't get overly positive or negative which would interfere with performance. You are a cool player who doesn't let things get to you, and are a calm presence.

3. You are aware when you leave your process, and can bring yourself back to your process.

4. You control the controllables, and let go of uncontrollables including errors and mistakes.

5. You play with confidence, and know how to control and channel your energy to win. You trust your process, believe in yourself, and don't give up.

6. You have physical and mental control and discipline, and consistently perform at a high level. Others can rely on you in clutch situations.

7. You are a performance leader that others emulate.

"The game ain't over till it's over."
– Yogi Berra

"We need a hit, so here I go."
– Joe DiMaggio

BASEBALL—LIFE STEP #3

FOCUS ON THE PROCESS
A GOLF STORY

Rory McIlroy's Process - In July 2014, Rory McIlroy won The Open Championship (British Open) and was declared "Champion Golfer of the Year." At age 25, he was the youngest to ever win 3 out of 4 of golf's modern major championships. All week, he talked about two simple mantras he used as trigger words for the shots he played. They were Process and Spot. "I just kept telling myself two words... "On my long shots I wanted to simply stick to my Process, make good decisions and make a good swing, and just keeping that so I wasn't thinking about the end result. And for my put, just focus on my spot: just pick a spot on the green and try to roll it over my spot. I wasn't thinking about the result, wasn't thinking about holing it. I just wanted to roll the ball over that spot. If it went in, great. If it didn't, then I'd try it the next hole." He kept his focus on executing his plan, and trusting that his practice would pay off. By focusing on near-term, activity-based targets, rather than worrying about predicting the end result, he was able to get the result he was aiming for all along. He didn't allow himself to get distracted with too much thinking while he was hitting the ball. McIlroy expounded on what the two words meant to him: "Staying in the process, make good mental decisions, make good swings, stay in the moment, stay focused, execute your game plan, stick to your game plan," McIlroy explained. "There's quite a lot of mental strength that goes on to not allow yourself to think about winning, or the result, or what it would mean for your career. You have to refrain from thinking about it because any sort of thought can derail you; a loss of concentration, a loss of focus...For me to play golf at this level, it's all mental. The physical capabilities are there. A lot of guys on tour can go out and shoot a 65 or 66 on any given day, but it's being able to do it when you need to and do it when the pressure is on, and I feel like I'm getting better at that."

Link to Baseball: *It's the same with hitting baseballs. Focus on seeing and hitting the ball in a certain spot of the strike zone, not thinking about hitting a double or triple, but simply getting the best opportunity to hit the ball squarely, and letting a good swing determine the result.*

BASEBALL–LIFE STEP #3

Nick Saban and Process - "Nick Saban, as coach of the University of Alabama football team, has brought Alabama to three national BCS championships (2009, 2011, 2012) and is considered by many to be the best coach in college football. He runs his entire life and program on a tightly packed schedule. There is very little downtime in his life. He runs high school football camps, coaches, evaluates, and recruits players, gives speeches, deals with player problems, and strategizes to win major championships. What separates him from the crowd is his approach to management and coaching. He focuses himself and everyone around him on the Process. The Process is a detailed program that each player must follow, keeping his players and coaches focused on execution rather than results. The focus on Process began at a game in November 1998 when he was the head coach at Michigan State and his unranked Spartans were to face the undefeated Ohio State team on the road. He told them that rather than worry about winning the game (which seemed like a long shot), they were going to focus on executing each play, one by one. Each player was to focus simply on executing the task they were responsible for during a given play, and not worry about the next play. He found they were looser, more relaxed, and played with more confidence.

In a huge upset win, Michigan State came from behind to win 28-24 against the reigning champions. He decided from then on to stop talking about the importance of winning, and to start focusing on this process-oriented approach to preparing and playing. He explained: 'I'm not naive enough to think that winning isn't important. But what that game made me realize is how much better it is for people not to worry about the opposition but to focus on executing and know if they do their job correctly, they're going to be successful, rather than thinking the other guy's going to determine the outcome.'" – Fortune, September 24, 2012.

BASEBALL-LIFE STEP #3

ACHIEVE GOALS

SET POSITIVE GOALS

PERFORM AT HIGH LEVEL

INTENTIONAL TRAINING

Confidence can be developed. Confidence comes from knowing that you can do something well, and then doing it well, which reinforces your belief that you can do it well. Lack of confidence comes from the worry that you are not up to the task. This worry is legitimate if you have not trained yourself intentionally, and you are not able to focus on the process, which will compromise your ability to perform at your best. The way you develop confidence, then, is by practicing and training with intention, focusing on the process, which results in performing at a high level, and builds your belief that you control your level of performance, creating true confidence within yourself that you are not only up to the task, but are able to compete with the best. *Legitimate confidence comes from having a process, practicing your process, and trusting your process.* The first thing that will happen when you hit a rough patch, and don't get the results you want, is monkey mind will want to override your process. This is because monkey mind is rendered useless when you have a process, and monkey mind does not like to be useless. You must *not* let monkey mind overthrow your process. You must stick to and follow your process, doing exactly what you've practiced. Confidence, by definition, comes from not doubting yourself or your process. It comes from trusting that you know and will do exactly what you need to do. Everything you need is already inside you.

FOCUS ON THE PROCESS

BASEBALL–LIFE STEP #3

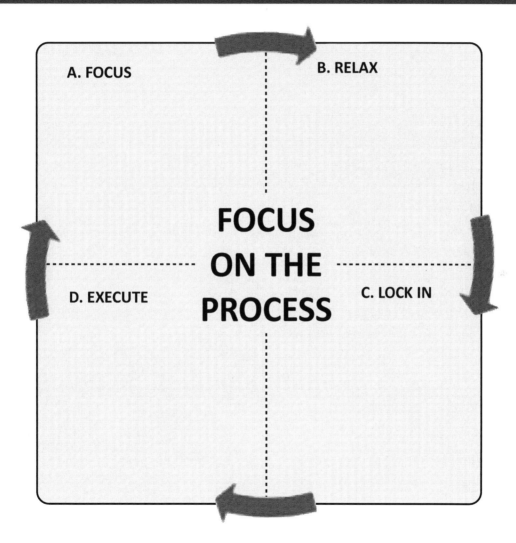

A. FOCUS

B. RELAX

FOCUS ON THE PROCESS

D. EXECUTE

C. LOCK IN

Create a customized plan for a specific action and how you will Focus on the Process, step by step.

BASEBALL IS A JOURNEY

You might think that
Baseball is about
winning the most games,
getting hits,
striking guys out,
stealing bases,
winning championships.
What you might not have considered is that
Baseball is played
through a whole, long season.
that the best of the best have
winning games and losing games,
hot streaks and slumps,
good times and bad times.
But the best of the best
aren't deterred as easily as average people.
The best of the best
believe in themselves,
are patient, persevere, never give up,
have a long term agenda.
The best of the best know
Baseball is a Journey
Not a Destination.
We hope this inspires you to
Lead Like a Champion.

PART 2

LEAD LIKE A CHAMPION

LEAD LIKE A CHAMPION

Steps #4,5,6 are about Leading Like A Champion

Part 2 is about managing your baseball career trajectory. It is organized in analogous fashion to Part 1. In order to play the game well, you must learn to operate like a champion, which means to Set Positive Goals, Train Intentionally, and Focus On The Process. In order to have a successful long-term baseball career, you must be able to manage your path forward, which means you must first Identify Your Vision (where you want to be in 5, 10, and 15 years), know what rules and guidelines will anchor your behaviors and choices through time (to be in integrity with yourself and your values), and Write Your Own Story (choose how your life and career unfold over time, as expected and unexpected things happen to you). Identifying your vision for the longer term horizon in Part 2 is analogous to setting positive goals at the operational level, because it creates a purpose and aim for your actions. Anchoring your behaviors and choices to your rules, morals, ethical values for the longer term horizon in Part 2 is analogous to training intentionally at the operational level, because it organizes your behaviors and conduct. And writing your own story in Part 2 is analogous to focusing on the process at the operational level, because it affects the quality and level of your performance, and makes you who you are. The difference between Part 1 and Part 2 is that Part 1 is about how you can perform at your highest level within a specific duration of time (e.g. the spring baseball season). In contrast, Part 2 is about managing your baseball career over the medium to long term, and how to make good medium-term decisions and choices such as what school to go to, what coach or team to play for, where to live, what to do during your "off" time, how to navigate the ups and downs of life. Part 3 is about how to transition from one season to the next as you cultivate your development and growth as a ball player and person. This depends on reaching for the next level, growing your self-awareness, and raising your knowledge and competency. So let's get started on Part 2 and taking personal leadership of your life and leading yourself like a champion. This is where we will talk about vision, integrity, and self-determination, which are the key qualities of a true leader.

	AIM	**PREPARE**	**EXECUTE**
OPERATE LIKE A CHAMPION	**1** Set Positive Goals	**2** Train Intentionally	**3** Focus on the Process
LEAD LIKE A CHAMPION	**4** Identify Your Vision	**5** Live By Your Rules	**6** Write Your Own Story
GROW LIKE A CHAMPION	**7** Reach For The Next Level	**8** Grow Self-Awareness	**9** Raise Your Game

Vision at age 15	in 5 years (age 20)	in 10 years (age 25)	in 15 years (age 30)	in 25 years (age 40)
Baseball	playing in D1	drafted in top 5 rounds, Majors by 24.	Playing ball in a men's leagues	coaching baseball
Education	get college degree	get an MBA at night	NA	NA
Career	finishing school	playing baseball	Start a business	Manager / VP in a company
Relationship	single	in a relationship	married	kids
Income & Wealth	$20,000 wealth	$400,000 wealth	$600,000 wealth	$1mm wealth

Your ability to Identify Your Vision in Step #4 is directly related to how well you operationalize Steps #1,2,3 in Part 1. If you are successful with training your body and mind, and focusing on the process and competing at a high level, you will be more likely to get a good college scholarship, and drafted out of college, which will affect your future baseball and career opportunities.

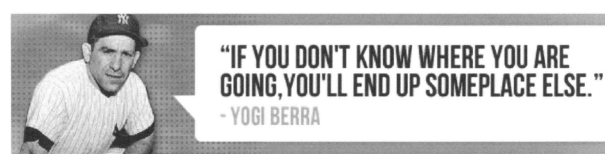

"IF YOU DON'T KNOW WHERE YOU ARE GOING, YOU'LL END UP SOMEPLACE ELSE."
- YOGI BERRA

BASEBALL—LIFE STEP #4

WHAT IS A "VISION"?

1) An idea based on a kernel of possibility that gets blown up into the best picture of what might be possible.
2) Something you see clearly, that you want to happen, and inspires and draws you towards it.
3) A North Star that helps you to fix your sights on something greater.

WHAT DOES IT MEAN TO "IDENTIFY YOUR VISION"?

1) To not just think about day to day things, but to look forward towards the future.
2) To consider how things would be if great things were to occur between now and the future.
3) To take the first step to imagining the future so that it can begin to happen today.

WHAT'S THE DIFFERENCE BETWEEN A GOAL AND A VISION?

1) A goal tends to be about near term outcomes, while a vision tends to be more long term.
2) A goal helps you improve and achieve a specific outcome, while a vision is more aspirational, inspirational, and may seem a bit "wild" to the average person.
3) The biggest difference is that a goal is realistic, while a vision doesn't seem controllable.

WHAT MAKES IT DIFFICULT TO IDENTIFY YOUR VISION?

1) It's easy to get caught up in life right now, and forget to think about the future.
2) The future may seem too far off and not really within your control.
3) The future can seem too fuzzy and impossible to articulate clearly.

WHY IS IT IMPORTANT TO WORK TO "IDENTIFY YOUR VISION"?

1) To be inspired to work hard, be focused, and do and become something great.
2) To have a picture of your future life that draws you forward.
3) To have a long run view, not just a short term perspective.

"The only person you are destined to become is the person you decide to be." – *Ralph Waldo Emerson*

"If you can dream it, you can achieve it." – *Zig Ziglar*

"I always wanted to be a major-league baseball player." – *Bryce Harper*

"Go confidently in the direction of your dreams. Live the life you have imagined." – *Henry David Thoreau*

"It's tough to make predictions, especially about the future."
– *Yogi Berra*

"Opportunity is missed by most people because it is dressed in overalls and looks like work." – *Thomas Edison*

"I'm a guy who just wanted to see his name in the lineup everyday. To me, baseball was a passion to the point of obsession." – *Brooks Robinson*

"I've always wanted to be the best in the world as a baseball player. So when I started to think about opening a business, it was with that mindset."
– *Curt Schilling*

1. Spend a week looking around you: the MLB players you aspire to be like, the kids at school you look up to, the guys on your travel team, their parents and families, your teachers, coaches, neighbors, community members. Is there any one who has a life that you'd really like for yourself? If so, go talk to them, or do some research to find out how they got where they are today. Get a sense for what's out there in the world, what the potential paths and opportunities are.

2. Then on a Sunday at 9pm, choose a quiet place, and close your eyes for 10 minutes. With your eyes closed, allow yourself to dream of your ideal future at age 25, within the realm of what's possible*. Allow yourself to dream in color, sounds, and details. Then open close your eyes and spend 15 minutes writing down this vision.
   i.   Where do you live?
   ii. What do you look like?
   iii. Who are you living with?
   iv. What are you doing in the mornings, afternoons, evenings?
   v.   What's the weather like?
   vi. Who are you doing stuff with?
   vii. How do you feel?
   viii.What kind of car do you drive?

3. Repeat the exercise, now imagining yourself at 40, within the realm of what's possible*.

4. Create two 16"x20" vision boards based on what you wrote and imagined, to help make your visions concrete and visual. Find images, words, quotes, photos that inspire you and represent your vision for yourself, and paste them onto your 2 vision boards (one for age 25 and one for age 40). Share your two vision boards with 2 close friends.

5. Now on a piece of paper, draw a picture connecting you today to you at ages 25 and 40, and put stepping stones along the path. Spend a week thinking about your visions and your stepping stones to your visions, and try to fill in these "stones" as they occur to you. These are the opportunities that will begin to move you towards your vision. (see p.68)

     * Stretch your imagination for what's possible beyond what you're used to, but not beyond what's physically possible. Making a lot of money is possible, but flying with wings is not.

You (40)

Jobs

Networks

MBA

You (25)

College

Summer Ball

Internships

Fitness Training

You (15)

BASEBALL–LIFE STEP #4

GO TO COLLEGE FIRST

For most ball players, setting a goal of getting good grades and a college scholarship makes more sense than going pro right away. Sure, if you are a first-round draft pick *and* get offered a $2mm+ signing bonus *and* are mature enough, maybe you go pro right away. But for most draftable 18 year olds, even if the scouts show lots of interest in you, and want to sign you out of high school, we think that going to college still makes better sense. Give yourself three years to mature, then re-enter the draft after junior year. Why? Let's say you go pro right away. Then you turn your signing bonus into a new car and you're off to rookie ball in Florida. You're in a barracks situation and half of your teammates don't speak English. Gone are your friends, family, girl friend and home cooking. Instead, you live on a small monthly salary and you're on your own to sink or swim. If you progress annually, from rookie ball, three levels of "A" ball, low, middle and high A, to double "AA" and triple "AAA," that's 5 years in the minors. But less than half of each team at each level will advance to the next year. If you don't continue to advance, you have no college and no baseball. On the other hand, if you turn down that out-of-high-school draft offer and accept a college scholarship to get a higher education and play baseball at the same time, you get to have your cake and eat it too. Playing on scholarship means someone is essentially paying you to play baseball, but you also get to receive a college education and degree. At 18, you give yourself time to mature, live in a dormitory with others your age, maintain contact with people back home, while continuing to get expert instruction, refine your work ethic, and be a part of the college experience. Your progress and playing time will depend on how much effort you put into the team and classroom. When you re-enter the draft, you will have had 3-4 years of education which nobody can take away from you, possibly a degree, and most likely get to start your pro career at a higher level, like AA level. If baseball suddenly were to end, you'd still have good options.

BASEBALL-LIFE STEP #4

The habit of identifying a vision for yourself as a ball player sets you up well for life. One way this habit can serve you well is with money. If you've developed the habit to dream big, have greater aspirations, perhaps even think a bit "wildly," identifying out-of-the-box possibilities and opportunities for yourself, fixing your sight on something that others might deem "impossible," then you will be in the habit of stretching yourself towards possibilities that others ignore, and that includes financially. It is only impossible if you believe it's impossible. If we stretch towards the impossible, we can surprise ourselves.

What is your vision for how much money you will make?
What is your vision for how much wealth you will have?
What is your commitment level to your financial vision?

MONEY VISION	STEPPING STONES
To make $100,000/year	• Identify possible career paths that would enable you to make this kind of money. • Get the education or experience needed to get on this career path. • Ask others how they manage to make this kind of money themselves.
To have a net worth of $1mm by age 40.	• Find a financial mentor or two. • Learn how wealthy people grew their wealth over time. • Learn to think like a wealthy person.
To contribute $10,000 per year to charities by age 40.	• Identify some charitable causes that really move you. • Begin making smaller charitable contributions, and grow this amount over time. • Learn how charitable giving grows your confidence and earning potential.

Practicing the art of identifying your vision, not only in baseball, but also with money, helps to establish this habit as a way to "Do Life." Identifying your vision is the first step to fixing your course and staying on course as you move forward in your life. Eventually, it'll be natural for you to look forward into the long-term future, as a way to create a strong directional anchor, for your life, relationships, career, and family, in the same way.

BASEBALL–LIFE STEP #4

YOU HAVE MASTERED STEP #4 IF...

1. You dare to think beyond the ordinary about what's possible for yourself and others.

2. You regularly take time to think about the medium and long-term future.

3. Your day-to-day actions are inspired by your long-term vision.

4. You naturally see opportunities and possibilities where others don't.

5. By seeing and taking advantage of opportunities, you make yourself "lucky."

6. Your visions tend to come true, because you believe and act as if they will come true.

7. You believe that dreams are possible, and inspire others to dream big.

"Vision is the art of seeing what is invisible to others."
– Jonathan Swift

"Where there is no vision, there is no hope." – George Washington Carver

"The only thing worse than being blind is having sight but no vision." – Helen Keller

"Leadership is the capacity to translate vision into reality." – Warren Bennis

What is your vision of yourself as a father/ mother?

As a father or mother, you are the leader of your family. The vision you possess for yourself, for your family, and for each of your children will leave a powerful imprint on your family. Remember that a vision is inspirational, aspirational, optimistic, and is a picture of something that resonates for a person or group about who they really could be. A vision is *not* something you make people do, but a picture that inspires people to do their best. The more clear and specific your vision of greatness, and the more committed you are to this picture of greatness, the more effective a leader you will be. This clear vision will influence all the choices and decisions you make, the investments you make, the way you conduct yourself, the language you use, and the attitudes you hold. What happens when you don't bother to identify any vision for yourself, your family, or your child? There will be 3 main consequences: 1) Rather than inspire your children and your family with hope and possibility, you will be constrained by cold, hard reality. 2) Rather than trying to reach for something greater, you will think that this is all that you can have. 3) Rather than lead by example and vision, you will be more passive and reactive. Overall, there will be less hope, less positivity, less inspiration, and less purpose. So, hopefully you are inspired to make the effort to master step #4 for yourself. The more you understand what step #4 really requires of you, the more you can help your son to identify and live into his own vision for himself. Step #4 is really about cultivating a habit of mind of positivity, and looking for and creating opportunities that conform to your idea of what's possible. The tricky thing about this vision thing is that, on the one hand, you want to be optimistic about what's possible, but on the other hand, it needs to be based on evidence that it is possible. If your son's vision is to be a major league baseball player, will you support him or tell him to forget about it? This will depend on your own vision for yourself and the kind of person you see yourself being.

BASEBALL–LIFE STEP #4

What is your vision as a high school baseball coach?

What might seem outside the realm of possible, but would be something you would want for yourself and your team anyways? Let's just say that at the beginning of the season, you've got a talented, but not unbelievably talented group of freshman boys. Certainly not the most talented and gifted bunch of boys that you've ever had. What vision might you have for yourself and your team this season and for the next 3 years? Remember that one of the big differences between a goal and a vision is that a goal is actionable, realistic, and within your control, while a vision is aspirational, a bit "wild" to the average eyes, and seemingly beyond your control. And why does Step #4 matter anyways, in the grand scheme of things? Because it is your vision of what's possible for you and these boys that will determine what immediate goals you set for yourself and for them. If you believe that you can only win a few games, then that is where you will be setting your sights, and how you will design your practices. If, however, you believe that your "unlikely" team can win the league championship as Juniors, then you will set your sights on a league championship, and this is what you will gear yourself and the team up for. This means that the "stepping stones" you leverage, the opportunities that you create, will be ones that steer you towards this larger aspiration. Sure, it doesn't seem "likely" that this scruffy bunch of boys could do it. But if you have a vision of a league championship anyways, then every single thing you do everyday will be informed by this vision, including the language you use, the positivity and hope you bring, the inspiration you give them, and your leadership style. You will work to develop your talent from low to high as completely as possible, because you know that you are going to need each and every team member to win that championship. You will teach them about mental attitude, mental discipline, confidence, strategy, and work on strength and speed conditioning, treat them like the championship team they are going to be. All because you have a vision that this is who and what they are!

BASEBALL-LIFE STEP #4

Vision at age 15	STEPPING STONES	in 10 years (age 25)	STEPPING STONES	in 25 years (age 40)
Baseball				
Education				
Career				
Relationship				
Income & Wealth				
Other?				

Take some time to consider and write down your vision for yourself 10 and 25 years out, and what some of the stepping stones and potential opportunities you might want to leverage to help you get to your particular vision.

	AIM	**PREPARE**	**EXECUTE**
OPERATE LIKE A CHAMPION	**1** Set Positive Goals	**2** Train Intentionally	**3** Focus on the Process
LEAD LIKE A CHAMPION	**4** Identify Your Vision	**5** Live By Your Rules	**6** Write Your Own Story
GROW LIKE A CHAMPION	**7** Reach For The Next Level	**8** Grow Self-Awareness	**9** Raise Your Game

BASEBALL-LIFE STEP #5

CONDUCT RULES

LANGUAGE RULES

YOUR RULES

YOUR RULES

HABIT RULES

MINDSET RULES

Your ability to <u>Live By Your Rules</u> in Step #5 is directly related to how well you <u>Identify your Vision</u> in Step #4. Because without a clear vision, you cannot have a clear commitment to realizing your vision which is what living by your rules is all about.

BASEBALL-LIFE STEP #5

WHAT IS "YOUR RULES"?

1) It is a set of values, principles, and standards (re: habits, mindset, language, conduct) that you have identified for yourself and that you hold yourself accountable to.

2) It is how you express your personal character, integrity, and self-respect.

3) It defines who you are, and what you stand for.

WHAT DOES IT MEAN TO "LIVE BY YOUR RULES"?

1) To conduct yourself everyday according to your personally defined rules.

2) To engage in principled, dignified, good behavior, with self-imposed self-control.

3) To commit yourself to realize your vision and dreams, and be the person you want to be.

WHY IS IT IMPORTANT TO "LIVE BY YOUR RULES"?

1) To have self-respect, clear boundaries, honor commitments, be consistent and disciplined.

2) To be capable of intentionally controlling your actions to keep yourself moving forward.

3) To hold yourself accountable to be your best, live up to your potential, realize your vision.

HOW DO YOU KNOW WHEN YOU AREN'T LIVING BY YOUR RULES?

1) When you find yourself changing direction all the time.

2) When you don't feel like you can gain traction and momentum to move forward in life.

3) When you feel unanchored, lost, and without purpose.

WHAT MAKES IT DIFFICULT TO LIVE BY YOUR RULES?

1) Rules are rules because they remind us about the boundaries we often want to cross.

2) It can be tempting to take short cuts and the easy way out, and hard to be accountable.

3) Commitment requires dedication and perseverance, and that can be hard for humans.

BASEBALL-LIFE STEP #5

"He who stands for nothing will fall for anything." – *Alexander Hamilton*

"Number one rule, attend to business." – *Lefty Grove*

"A bad attitude is like a flat tire. If you don't change it, you'll never go anywhere."

"We are what we repeatedly do. Excellence, then, is not an act but a habit." – *Aristotle*

"Men's natures are alike; it is their habits that separate them." – *Confucius*

"The difference between who you are and who you want to be... is what you do."

"Go 24 hours without complaining. (Not even once.) Then watch how your life starts changing!" – *Katrina Mayer*

"We first make our habits, and then our habits make us."
– *John Dryden*

"Unsuccessful people use their words to describe their situation. Successful people use their words to direct their situation."

"Life is hard if you live it the easy way and it is easy if you live it the hard way." – *Kekich Credo*

BASEBALL–LIFE STEP #5

LIVE BY YOUR RULES

The first thing you need to do if you are serious about living by your rules and staying on your best path is to identify and adhere to some fundamental MINDSET RULES for yourself. Most of us are not aware of how powerful our thoughts are. How our life today is a direct result of our past and present beliefs about ourselves, and how we think.

E. STAY IN THE MOMENT: Let go of the past. Don't worry about the future.

D. CONFIDENCE: Believe in myself. Assume I'm going to hit a line drive, make the catch, throw a strike.

C. BE POSITIVE: Look on the bright side and have a good attitude.

YOUR RULES

YOUR RULES

B. FIRST THINGS FIRST: Prioritize and focus on what's most important right now.

A. KNOW MYSELF: Always be clear what I want.

1. MINDSET RULES

79

BASEBALL–LIFE STEP #5

The second thing you need to do if you are serious about living by your rules and staying on your best path is to identify, adhere to, and enforce some fundamental HABIT RULES. Habits are routines we do over and over that essentially make us who we are. Give yourself 3 weeks to develop a habit, so that it becomes a real part of your everyday life. Here are some examples.

E. <u>GET 8 HOURS SLEEP/NIGHT</u>

D. <u>EAT HEALTHY FOOD, NO SMOKING OR DRUGS</u>

C. <u>MEDITATE 10 MINUTES/DAY</u>

YOUR RULES

YOUR RULES

B. <u>50 SWINGS PER DAY</u>

A. <u>CONDITIONING, SPEED, STRENGTH, FLEXIBILITY TRAINING 5 DAYS/WEEK</u>

2. HABIT RULES

Good Habits / Bad Habits

BASEBALL—LIFE STEP #5

LIVE BY YOUR RULES

The third thing you need to do if you are serious about living by your rules and staying on your best path is to identify, adhere to, and enforce some LANGUAGE RULES. Words have incredible power over us. We use language to label our experiences. The words we use affect not only how we feel and behave, but how we experience and direct our life, and thus the quality of our life.

E. <u>GIVE THANKS</u>: Express appreciation and gratitude to teammates, coaches, friends, and loved ones at least 1x/day.

D. <u>APOLOGIZE</u>: Take responsibility and quickly apologize when you say something hurtful or do something wrong.

C. <u>SAY IT WITH CONVICTION</u>: Don't say I'll "try" to do something, say I "will" do it.

B. <u>BE HONEST</u>: Stay real and tell yourself and others the truth.

A. <u>BE SPECIFIC</u>: Hold yourself accountable with your language by being specific about what you will do, how, and when.

YOUR RULES

YOUR RULES

3. LANGUAGE RULES

The fourth thing you need to do if you are serious about living by your rules and staying on your best path is to identify and adhere to some CONDUCT RULES. The bottom line is that our actions express our character and integrity, so we must establish rock-bottom behavior rules that we hold ourselves accountable for.

E. <u>BE A LEADER</u>: Be a role model, support and encourage teammates.

D. <u>BRING MY "A" GAME</u>: Everyone counts on me to do my best, be mentally alert, bring my best attitude and best performance.

C. <u>SELF-CONTROL</u>: Play under control, don't get knocked off course by hurtful words, mistakes, or bad luck. Learn from mistakes, but don't be discouraged by them.

B. <u>HUSTLE</u>: Always hustle. Hustle onto the field, run to first on a walk, run out grounders, flyballs, dropped third strikes, charge ground balls, hustle to catch foul balls.

A. <u>EXECUTE THE BASICS</u>: Put the ball in play, catch the ball, make the play, hit the cutoff, throw strikes, move the runner, get down in the dirt, don't swing at bad pitches, don't follow a bad play with another bad play.

YOUR RULES

YOUR RULES

4. CONDUCT RULES

BASEBALL–LIFE STEP #5

LIVE BY YOUR RULES

YOU HAVE MASTERED STEP #5 IF...

1. You respect yourself and respect others.

2. You've developed good habits, a positive mindset, encouraging language, and productive and pro-active behaviors.

3. You do not shy away from commitment.

4. You do what you say - you are a man of your words and don't break your promises.

5. You are a man of integrity and character.

6. You are disciplined, self-controlled, and live by your rules.

7. People can count on you because you are fair, ethical, and have good judgment.

LIFE RULES
BASEBALL RULES
CLASSROOM RULES
Be Ready To Learn
Say Please & Thank You
DREAM BIG
Keep Hands To Yourself
BE RESPECTFUL
Do Your Best
Take Risks & Make Mistakes
Raise Your Hand
FOLLOW DIRECTIONS
Work Hard

BASEBALL–LIFE STEP #5

The habit of living by your rules as a ball player sets you up well for life. One way this habit can serve you well is in friendships. If you've really learned how to live by your rules, it should be easy for you to extend this habit to being a good friend.

What are your rules in friendships?
Why are these rules important for the friendship?
How do these rules support and enhance the friendship?

FRIENDSHIP	RULES
Be Punctual	• I will not be punctual. If I will be late by more than 5 minutes, I will let them know.
Keep Confidentiality	• I will honor their confidentiality, and not share their private information with others.
Be Reliable	• I will do what I say. For example, I will return money that I owe on time, and I will be reliable and trustworthy in doing what I say I will do.
Be Honest	• I will be honest and tell them the truth, so that I am trustworthy and believable.

Practicing the art of living by your rules, not only in baseball, but also in friendship helps you to be a person of character and integrity. Living by your rules makes you someone that others can count on and trust.

BASEBALL-LIFE STEP #5

What rules do you abide by as a parent?

Many parents want to be buddies with their kids and are reluctant to set and enforce real rules with their children, especially as they become teenagers who push back and develop attitude. This leads to disorder, drama, and poor attitude by kids, and makes parenting even more challenging and frustrating. We also know parents who are hot-heads and aren't really helping their sons be the best that they could be. The best thing we can do for our ball players is set some clear rules for everyone in the family, including ourselves. With clear, but fair rules, and clear consequences, everyone can relax and do what they need to do. Here are six *"P" Rules for Parents* we believe foster good character and behavior:

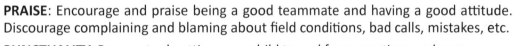

PRAISE: Encourage and praise being a good teammate and having a good attitude. Discourage complaining and blaming about field conditions, bad calls, mistakes, etc.

PUNCTUALITY: Be punctual getting your child to and from practices and games.

PATIENCE: Be patient with your son. Imagine that your son is climbing a ladder, and sometimes he might miss a rung, but the important thing is that he keeps climbing.

POSITIVITY: The more positive and engaged you are, the more positive and engaged your son will be.

PERSPECTIVE: Keep your perspective and remember that baseball is a game of dealing with failure. Even the best players make twice as many outs as hits. Focus on your son's progress rather than performance. If he is making progress, working hard, keeping up his grades, and coming along, that's the most important thing.

PREVENTION: Prevent your player from failing to make grades by monitoring his school performance, periodically checking the teachers' reports during the school year, making sure he's attending classes, handing in homework, studying for tests.

BASEBALL—LIFE STEP #5

To be honest, I have had a couple of kids who didn't act so well on the road and it cost us the opportunity to go all the way. I can't deny it. It happened early in our program. But it never happened again. Player, coach and parental conduct is an intricate part of the whole travel experience and is what you'll be remembered for. In more than a dozen World Series experiences, with one exception, the West Covina California Dukes Baseball team has had a stellar performance on and off the field. And I credit the parents for much of the players' performance success and their exemplary conduct on and off the field. This is a big deal with our coaching staff and to our program credit; we have won several sportsmanship awards. The travel experience affords most kids their first out of state and out of region travel experience and this is all by itself, worth the commitment. Here are the 10 Dukes Baseball rules we insisted be followed with consistency by our players:

1. All Dukes players are encouraged to attain academic excellence in the classroom, with a goal to attain college admittance and higher education. Books first and then baseball.

2. All Dukes players will be dressed in proper baseball attire at all practices and games. Shirts tucked in, hats on straight.

3. All Dukes players will stow their baseball bag or gear under the dugout bench or snapped on the fence, not on the open floor or near a gate.

4. All Dukes players and coaches will leave the dugout and field area in the same or better condition than which they found it. Clean up follows every practice and game.

5. All players will pick up a dead ball on the ground with their throwing hand. The purpose is to get into the habit of doing this and not reaching with the glove, which often falls short.

6. All Dukes players will swing their bat 50 times a night, at home, throughout the season; and all pitchers will do their balance drills at home, throughout the season.

7. The Dukes coaching staffs will teach proper baseball as outlined in our 5 baseball rules. Thus, from team to team and year to year, player adjustment is minimal.

8. The Dukes coaches will teach pitchers proper quick leg move and eliminate the slide-step habit.

9. The Dukes coaches will teach and utilize the "42" – two-strike adjustment to all players and practice it weekly. A ball in play has a good chance to get away.

10. All Dukes players, coaches and fans will address the umpire as Mr. Umpire, on and off the field. Yes, this may seem like a tough one but it pays off in the long run.

– By Duke DeFrates, founder of the Dukes Baseball Travel Team in West Covina.

BASEBALL-LIFE STEP #5

LIVE BY YOUR RULES

MINDSET RULES	Reasons	Consequences
1.		
2.		
3.		
HABIT RULES	Reasons	Consequences
1.		
2.		
3.		
LANGUAGE RULES	Reasons	Consequences
1.		
2.		
3.		
CONDUCT RULES	Reasons	Consequences
1.		
2.		
3.		

* Write down some rules that will help you improve your baseball game and your school grades, as well as the specific reason for following the rule, and the consequence you will give yourself if you fail to adhere to your rule.

I'm just a kid chasing perfection in a game built on failure.

– Twitter quote

	AIM	PREPARE	EXECUTE
OPERATE LIKE A CHAMPION	1 Set Positive Goals	2 Train Intentionally	3 Focus on the Process
LEAD LIKE A CHAMPION	4 Identify Your Vision	5 Live By Your Rules	6 Write Your Own Story
GROW LIKE A CHAMPION	7 Reach For The Next Level	8 Grow Self-Awareness	9 Raise Your Game

BASEBALL–LIFE STEP #6

"Storytelling is like fortune-telling. The act of choosing a certain story determines the probability of future outcomes."
– Michael Margolis

You (40)

WRITE YOUR OWN STORY & GET BACK ON TRACK

Factors that could cause you to veer off track:
Injury
Accident
Illness
Rejection
Bad Slump
Harsh Media
Divorce
Tragedy

You (15)

BASEBALL-LIFE STEP #6

WRITE YOUR OWN STORY

WHAT IS A "STORY"?
1) It is a narrative with a beginning, middle, and end.
2) There is a protagonist who the audience cares about.
3) Typically, the protagonist encounters a problem, suffers and experiences pain, enlists support, does something to solve the problem, overcomes, and emerges victorious.

WHAT ARE THE 5 MAIN COMPONENTS OF A STORY?
1) The setting or context
2) The protagonist and other characters
3) The problem that the protagonist encounters
4) What the protagonist does to overcome his/her problem (the action / plot)
5) The story ending where the protagonist has resolved his issue

WHAT DOES IT MEAN TO "WRITE YOUR OWN STORY"?
1) To organize a sequence of experiences, and explain how things got to be the way they are.
2) To choose and determine how your story turns out, as the author of your own story.
3) To take an active role in cultivating your identity, your intangibles, who you are.

WHY IS IT IMPORTANT TO "WRITE YOUR OWN STORY"?
1) To overcome difficulty, cope with setbacks and challenges, and control your narrative.
2) To respond to the uncontrollable, unpredictable ups and downs with a sense of purpose.
3) To be aware of your life as a journey and series of "tests" that challenge you to grow.

WHAT HAPPENS IF YOU DON'T "WRITE YOUR OWN STORY"?
1) It will be harder to bounce back from seeming failure and suffering, and reinvent yourself.
2) You will have trouble making meaning of your experiences, challenges, and efforts.
3) You will not develop a sense of being in control of your life's journey.

BASEBALL-LIFE STEP #6

WRITE YOUR OWN STORY

QUOTES

"The beautiful thing about baseball is that anything can happen. It's like life in that way. As soon as you think you have it all figured out, something happens that makes you realize you know nothing. The only thing that's guaranteed is that it will be an exciting ride." – *Alyssa Milano*

"Babe Ruth was just this magnificent human being. And a really good story because he was this kid who grew up essentially as an orphan, had a tough life, and then he became the most successful player ever." – *Bill Bryson*

"Eighty percent of the people who hear (your troubles) don't care and the other twenty percent are glad you're having them" – *Tommy Lasorda, Dodgers*

"You have to understand that life and baseball are littered with all kinds of obstacles and problems along the way. You have to learn to overcome them to be successful in life." – *Dave Winfield*

"The two most important days in your life are the day you are born and the day you find out why." – *Mark Twain*

"Sometimes you have a plan and things happen that are unexpected. You've got to keep pushing. Life is not going to stop. You have to figure it out."
– *Alex Mascarenas - Former UCLA football player now playing baseball.*

"In sports and in life, we drastically underestimate the role of luck - how unusually good or bad performances typically involve some fortune or misfortune." – *Professor Gary Smith, Standard Deviations*

BASEBALL-LIFE STEP #6

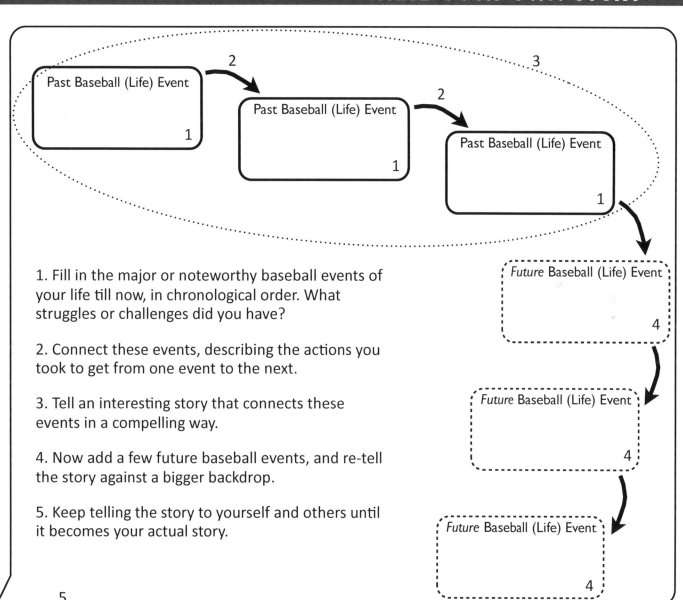

1. Fill in the major or noteworthy baseball events of your life till now, in chronological order. What struggles or challenges did you have?

2. Connect these events, describing the actions you took to get from one event to the next.

3. Tell an interesting story that connects these events in a compelling way.

4. Now add a few future baseball events, and re-tell the story against a bigger backdrop.

5. Keep telling the story to yourself and others until it becomes your actual story.

BASEBALL-LIFE STEP #6

Step #6 acknowledges that while we might be diligently doing our best, life can throw us unexpected curve balls that catch us by surprise, even knock us off course. Step #6 is about responding effectively to the surprises and challenges that life throws our way, and harnessing our intangibles. Stories are imaginative interpretations of who we are. We typically begin to create our stories of ourselves in our teens as we move past our childhood of learning the rules, learning to belong, learning how to get attention and please others. In adolescence, we are beginning to figure out who we are, and what makes us tick. Writing your story is about consciously cultivating the story of who you are, what you are about, and expressing your intangibles of character, resilience, grit, perseverance. One of the best ways to familiarize yourself with how to write a story is by learning of the stories of other baseball players, reading biographies, and following players in the news today. Most stories, you'll come to realize, are stories of underdogs and heros. On the next page is an example of a player who writes the story of his life, as a way to make meaning of his larger baseball experience and life trajectory. It's a story we can all related to of a ball player who was frequently underestimated, but persevered and proved that he was better than people thought, and came up strong when it counted. Having a larger story enabled the ball player to understand the larger context of his experience, so that he didn't feel tempted to give up when the going got tough. He didn't get down on himself when he had a bad performance. Because he had a bigger story of his life as a ball player, he understood that there would inevitably be periods of his life when things would be more challenging, and it would be at those points that he would have to bear down, do the hard work, be humble, and stay strong for the fight.

> "I always look at baseball like the stock market. You don't look at it every day. When it's a good stock, after a long season, it's going to be there." - Alex Rodriguez

"The harder I practice, the luckier I get." - Gary Player, winner of 9 major golf championships

BASEBALL-LIFE STEP #6

WRITE YOUR OWN STORY

Past Baseball (Life) Event
Little League
7-12 yrs old;
All-Star Teams;
Ok, not the best 1

2 *found a travel team*

Past Baseball (Life) Event
Travel Ball Team;
Most Improved Player
National Tournaments 1

2 *worked really hard*

3 *had some doubters,*
persevered, improved

Past Baseball (Life) Event
High School Team;
Leader and one of
the better players 1

Future Baseball (Life) Event
D1 College Ball
Freshman year
challenging 4

Future Baseball (Life) Event
Junior Year,
1st or 2nd round
draft pick 4

Future Baseball (Life) Event
Play in Minors for 3 yrs;
Play in Majors for 3 yrs;
Lots of ups and downs 4

"When I was 10, I was not the best ball player in Little League. There were a handful of other boys that the coaches felt were better ball players, and it was clear they were the "favored" ones. But I persevered, grew taller, and by high school, had become a leader, and one of the better players on the team. But on my summer travel ball team, I again faced a situation of being under-estimated and undervalued, while some other boys seemed to be the "chosen ones." But because I had faced a similar situation before, I didn't let it get to me. I focused on improving myself and growing at my pace. I imagine that by senior year of high school, I will be a top recruit whom lots of D1 colleges court. But when I get to college, I'll have to prove myself all over again. But I will persevere, put in the work and have the right perspective and attitude. I imagine that by the end of my junior year in college, I will be a first or second round draft pick in the MLB."

5 *Overall Story: developed a passion for the game,*
developed an identity as a ball player, proved my
grit, determination, resilience, and belief in myself.

Evan Longoria Wrote His Own Story

When Evan was 18 years old, he was completely overlooked, and was not even recruited to play college ball. He was considered too small and weak. But with hard work, he was able to be a top draft pick three years later. He went to Rio Hondo Junior College and then Long Beach State. At Long Beach State, he developed his Mental Game. It was not easy. He had to learn to train his mental skills, and control his focus and concentration. He also had to train intentionally to become stronger and faster. At Long Beach State, under the coaching of a sports psychologist, Ken Ravizza, he learned to stick with his approach, stay in the game, not worry about the result, bring a sense of calm, and have faith in the process. He developed a highly honed mental approach to the game. He learned to be present in the moment, forget about the last at bat, and just take things one pitch at a time. He wrote his story by determining his desired story ending, and focusing on the actions he needed to take to make this outcome come true. He trained diligently on the fundamentals, and developed his mental game to be able to focus and concentrate. Evan Longoria was the third overall pick in the 2006 MLB Draft, and after two seasons in the minors, played for the Tampa Bay Rays in the majors. He was named 2008 Rookie of the Year, and was the Tampa Bay Rayss all-time RBI leader in 2014. He is now considered one of the best third basemen in the game, is considered the face of the franchise, and has signed a 10-year, $100 million contract extension through 2022!

"You just can't beat the person who never gives up."
– Babe Ruth

BASEBALL—LIFE STEP #6

WRITE YOUR OWN STORY

Mike Lamb Wrote His Own Story

Mike was a Dukes baseball player, and one of the first Dukes Scholar-Athletes in 1989. He was a good hitter, but had some difficulty in the field, and was not considerd the best player on the team. However, at Bishop Amat High School, with growth and maturity, Mike reached the next tier of skill. Mike, a second baseman with the Dukes, and a third baseman in high school, was a walk on at Cal State Fullerton. He was red-shirted his first year, rode the bench for a year, then got a chance to play, and made the most of it. He earned a college scholarship, won an NCAA title, and was named MVP as a Junior. Mike was then drafted by the Texas Rangers in the 7th round of the 1997 draft as a third baseman. After 3 years in the minors, he debuted for the Texas Rangers in April 2000. He had a 9-year MLB career batting average of .276, 69 homeruns, and 349 RBIs. He played for the Texas Rangers for 3 years, the Houston Astros for 3 years, the Twins, Brewers, and played first base for the Marlins, ending in July 2010. He is now married with 3 children. He wasn't the biggest or the best when he was younger, but he dedicated himself to being the best player he could be. He ignored the naysayers and doubters, and went to the top.

"Erase the Doubt."

"The key to having a long career in the major leagues is competitive fire and confidence. It's more important than talent, more important than what round you get drafted in."

– Michael Young

Michael Young Wrote His Own Story

Michael went to Bishop Amat High School. While he was an outstanding short stop, his best friend Steve was considered even better, and so he played center field. Both Michael and his best friend were named All-CIF player, and both were granted full-ride scholarships to UCSB. But while his best friend went pro right after high school, Michael decided to go to college, even though he was drafted by the Baltimore Orioles. In college, he played short stop, and was an All-American at UCSB. Then, after Junior year, he was drafted by the Toronto Blue Jays. After several seasons in the minor leagues with the Blue Jays, he was traded to the Texas Rangers, where he played short stop until Alex Rodriguez, from the Seattle Mariners, was signed. Then Michael had to shift to second base. But after 3 years, Alex was traded to the NY Yankees, and Michael became their short stop for the next 5 years. Then he played for the Phillies and the Dodgers till 2014. His teammates said, "He was just a great teammate to have around." Now Michael is the assistant General Manager of the Texas Rangers. Since he was a young boy, Michael loved baseball, and was persistent and determined to succeed in baseball. He wrote his own story.

BASEBALL-LIFE STEP #6

WRITE YOUR OWN STORY

YOU HAVE MASTERED STEP #6 IF...

1. You have weaved a bigger story for yourself overall, and playing baseball.

2. You naturally listen for the stories of other players.

3. You love to hear stories of hardship, resilience, and success of pro athletes of all sports.

4. You recognize the inherent up-and-down nature of the game of baseball.

5. You don't let yourself get deterred by a particular "down" moment in your overall path.

6. You see the bigger journey of yourself with baseball, and your overall life trajectory.

7. You spend a decent amount of time thinking about your future story line, and how it is consistent with your past and present situation.

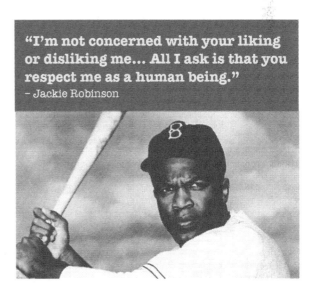

"I'm not concerned with your liking or disliking me... All I ask is that you respect me as a human being."
– Jackie Robinson

"He led America by example. He reminded our people of what was right and he reminded them of what was wrong. I think it can be safely said today that Jackie Robinson made the United States a better nation." – Gene Budig

BASEBALL-LIFE STEP #6

WRITE YOUR OWN STORY

As a parent of a baseball player, we are learning and growing right along side our ball player, the whole way. A baseball player is not born overnight, but made over several long years. By the time a boy is playing as a high school senior, he has likely played 12+ years, 1000+ games, and 6000+ hours. For parents, that translates to thousands of hours of baseball watching, thousands of gallons of gas driving them to and from practice, washing their clothes, preparing food for them, buying equipment, paying for coaches, fundraising, and getting worked up about games and how your son and his team did. But most importantly, it translates to learning to handle the ups and downs. Most of us have probably had to learn to manage our own frustration, competitiveness, or disappointment. And most of us have probably had to deal with negative and/or cutthroat parents and coaches as well. What it helps us to realize is that the best thing we can do as parents is to learn to calm down and see the bigger picture. A win or loss never is never as important as it seems in the moment. Being able to have a bigger perspective helps us to weather the ups and downs and stay positive for our boys. How many of the most successful athletes and coaches were under-rated, under-estimated, or under-respected, but found their success? Tom Brady, Michael Jordan, Pete Carroll, Evan Longoria. Learning the story of other pro athletes, and what they had to deal with, the doubters, naysayers, haters, the rejections, fighting for playing time, recovering from injuries, gives you perspective. Sometimes taking time away from the game is the best remedy. This gives us and our boys the time to write our own stories, from a distance. Crafting a story can be the best way to reset and rejuvenate the spirit. The stories we believe and tell can be one of the most powerful things we do to support our sons on their journeys.

"If your motivation is to win another national championship, it's not fun. It's too much stress, and you're focusing on the wrong things. It's not about the crystal ball. **It's about the players. It's about the journey.**" - Nick Saban.

BASEBALL–LIFE STEP #6

WRITE YOUR OWN STORY COACH'S CORNER

It took me 3 tries at the 14U AABC Sandy Koufax World Series before I discovered what it took to win. I openly admit it. In previous efforts with quality teams, we had come up short, runner-up twice. In the off-season, I racked my brain trying to evaluate what we did wrong and/or what else we needed to do to win it. I knew it wasn't the player's fault and that it lay with something that I had not done to prepare them for this last hurdle. Each year, it was an adventure and a learning experience. Then, following another West Regional title, nearing our next World Series, I decided that the missing ingredient was right in front of my nose. We had dotted all the i's and crossed all the t's, just like every other year, but in each previous effort, something negative always came up. The first was seeding against Texas, the Southwest region champion and playing our first game at 9:00 AM in Houston, 7:00 AM California time. The time difference, 110° heat and humidity knocked us out. The next also-ran performance was the result of a home umpiring job, which cost us a crucial semi-final game. The third was some combination of the above. I was responsible for not seeing the hiccups in advance and bridging the potholes. On our next trip, I decided that "no matter what – we will remain positive" for the whole tournament. I would not let the weather, a bracketing switch, an umpire, or the other team bring us down. If you expect to win it, and we did, then you have to trust yourself and the team. Every player has what it takes to excel inside of him or her already, so play that card and stay positive. The collective best will come through. You've taught all year, played a lot of games, come a long way, so why in the world should anyone think negatively at this point? When a coach is negative, it bleeds down to the kids. It wasn't easy to remain positive, and there were a couple possible negative snags, but we stayed positive and won. And we followed with another World Series title the next year in New Jersey. Everything we needed to be successful was already inside of us, so I just had to let it out. I had to believe and follow my own words. However, not long after winning our second title, I realized that the most important aspect of our program was the preparation and advancement of our graduates, and their high school and college futures.

– By Duke DeFrates, founder of the Dukes Baseball Travel Team in West Covina

BASEBALL–LIFE STEP #6

WRITE YOUR OWN STORY

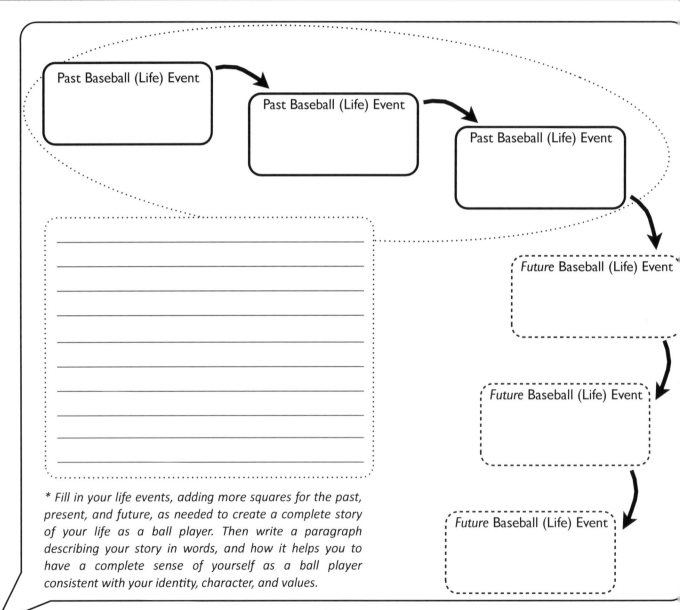

Past Baseball (Life) Event

Past Baseball (Life) Event

Past Baseball (Life) Event

Future Baseball (Life) Event

Future Baseball (Life) Event

Future Baseball (Life) Event

* *Fill in your life events, adding more squares for the past, present, and future, as needed to create a complete story of your life as a ball player. Then write a paragraph describing your story in words, and how it helps you to have a complete sense of yourself as a ball player consistent with your identity, character, and values.*

BASEBALL–LIFE STEP #6

WRITING YOUR STORY

PROGRESS FORWARD

IDENTIFY YOUR VISION

You have control of your life. You are in the driver's seat when you identify where you want to go, identify your vision, and then commit to this vision by following your rules, and stay on course by writing your story, especially in response to the ups and downs of life, the uncontrollable and unpredictable course of events that you had no way to anticipate ahead of time. Because baseball is a game of perfection played by imperfect humans, it is absolutely critical to develop the resilience to weather the ups and downs, both at the micro level, but also at the macro level of your life. Why do we devote a whole 3 Steps to How to Lead Like A Champion? Because without resilience, it is all too easy to crumble in the face of seeming failure. But if you have a vision, something that inspires and motivates you, and you follow your rules, and continue to write your story, as you overcome the odds, and the closed doors, and personal difficulties, even tragedies, then you are bound to succeed, because you have developed the skills to bounce back, and never let the world tell you something is impossible. Steps #4,5,6 give you the formula for following your dreams. Champions lead themselves, and don't let others define how their lives turn out, because they put themselves in the driver seat of their own life. Leaders know where they want to go, and hold steady towards their North Star.

STAY ON COURSE

FOLLOW YOUR RULES

WRITE YOUR STORY

BASEBALL IS LIFE

It is said that if the
great white shark
stops swimming,
it will die.
If a leg is in a cast,
the muscles atrophy.
When we become complacent.
We don't feel the need
to do anything different.
But when we stop
challenging ourselves,
in baseball or in life,
we can't expect improvement.
All we can expect is status quo,
and hopefully not going backwards.
We certainly cannot expect to
reach new, higher levels.
Baseball, like life, requires us
to keep challenging ourselves,
to keep exercising our muscles and minds,
and stretching our hearts.

We hope you will continue to
Grow Like a Champion.

PART 3

GROW LIKE A CHAMPION

GROW LIKE A CHAMPION

Steps #7,8,9 are about Growing Like A Champion

Part 3 is about becoming adept at change, growth, and improving yourself. It is about raising your game and becoming even better at what you do. If you become stagnant, and stop learning and growing, then pretty soon, people will pass you by. Part 3 is organized in analogous fashion to Parts 1 and 2. In order to play the game well, you must learn to Operate Like a Champion, which means to Set Positive Goals, Train Intentionally, and Focus On The Process. In order to have a successful long term baseball career, you must be able to Identify Your Vision, Live By Your Rules, and Write Your Own Story. And in order to Grow Like a Champion, you must be able to adapt to increasingly higher levels of play, which requires that you Reach For The Next Level, Grow Self-Awareness, and Raise Your Game. Reaching For The Next Level in Part 3 is analogous to Setting Positive Goals at the operational level in Part 1, and Identifying Your Vision at the long-term level in Part 2, because these Steps help you to set your sights on something greater. Growing Self-Awareness in Part 3 is analogous to Training Intentionally at the operational level in Part 1, and Living By Your Rules at the long-term level in Part 2, because these Steps help you to anchor and solidify your new behaviors. And Raising Your Game in Part 3 is analogous to Focusing on the Process at the operational level in Part 1, and Writing Your Own Story in Part 2, because this is where the rubber meets the road and you actually implement the new aim and determine the quality of your performance, journey, and growth. The difference between Parts 1, 2, and 3 is that while Part 1 is about performing well within a specific duration of time, and Part 2 is about navigating your journey, Part 3 is about change and growth, taking on new challenges, making mistakes, learning by doing, being uncomfortable as you learn new skills and techniques, playing under greater pressure where the stakes are higher. So let's get started on Part 3. We will explore how to be a continual learner, develop a growth mindset, grow and improve, learn to learn, be adept at change, be more observant, self-aware, and masterful, which are the key ingredients to Growing Like a Champion.

	AIM	**PREPARE**	**EXECUTE**
OPERATE LIKE A CHAMPION	**1** Set Positive Goals	**2** Train Intentionally	**3** Focus on the Process
LEAD LIKE A CHAMPION	**4** Identify Your Vision	**5** Live By Your Rules	**6** Write Your Own Story
GROW LIKE A CHAMPION	**7** Reach For The Next Level	**8** Grow Self-Awareness	**9** Raise Your Game

BASEBALL-LIFE STEP #7

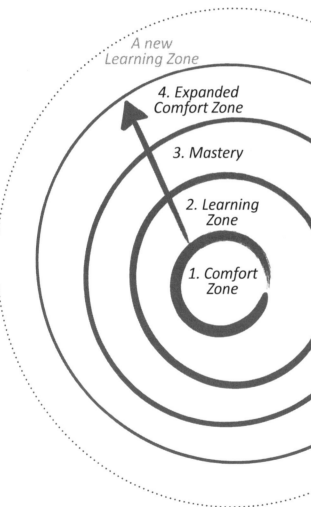

A new Learning Zone

4. Expanded Comfort Zone

3. Mastery

2. Learning Zone

1. Comfort Zone

The process of GROWTH is continual. It goes like this:

Acknowledge you're in a **Comfort Zone** where things are easy, and you don't have to try hard, but things feel a bit stale and unstimulating.

Step #7 is about Reaching For the Next Level by moving to a **Learning Zone**, which is outside your comfort zone, and becoming comfortable with being uncomfortable.

Step #8 is about Growing Your Self-Awareness, particularly in the *Learning Zone*, so that you can make substantive new improvements here.

Step #9 is about Raising Your Game and developing **Mastery** at the next level. Looking back, you will notice a big jump in your capabilities and thinking abilities.

When you get used to this higher level of play, you will move to an **Expanded Comfort Zone**, and need to repeat Steps #7,8,9 to keep growing.

BASEBALL-LIFE STEP #7

REACH FOR THE NEXT LEVEL

WHAT IS THE "NEXT LEVEL"?

1) There are many possible ways to define the "next level."

2) The next level could be varsity, or college, or playing in the minors or majors.

3) It could also be about the next level of physical or mental mastery.

WHAT DOES IT MEAN TO "REACH FOR THE NEXT LEVEL"?

1) To identify the necessary changes in your current level of play that you will need to make.

2) To begin to intentionally and deliberately prepare oneself to play at that next level.

3) To seek out the support and resources that you will need today to prepare yourself.

WHY IS IT IMPORTANT TO "REACH FOR THE NEXT LEVEL"?

1) Because it keeps you sharp and helps you maintain your competitive edge.

2) Because continual challenge is the only thing that develops true mastery.

3) Because life is dynamic, and resting on your laurels means others will pass you by.

WHAT ARE THE STEPS OF "REACHING FOR THE NEXT LEVEL"?

1) First, an awareness that you are in a "Comfort Zone."

2) Second, knowing when it's the right time to push yourself to a "Learning Zone."

3) Third, developing "Mastery At The Next Level."

4) Fourth, experiencing an "Expanded Comfort Zone" as you gain mastery at this higher level.

WHAT HAPPENS IF YOU DON'T "REACH FOR THE NEXT LEVEL"?

1) You will become complacent and not work hard.

2) You will lose your competitive edge that is developed by reaching higher.

3) You will stop prematurely before you've realized your fullest potential.

"Challenges are what make life interesting and overcoming them is what makes life meaningful." – *Joshua J. Marine*

"Failure is not failure, unless it is failure to change." – *John Wooden*

"You can't be afraid to make errors! You can't be afraid to be naked before the crowd, because no one can ever master the game of baseball, or conquer it. You can only challenge it." – *Lou Brock*

"The difference between a successful person and others is not a lack of strength, not a lack of knowledge, but rather a lack of will" – *Vince Lombardi*

"Progress is impossible without change, and those who cannot change their minds cannot change anything." – *George Bernard Shaw*

"The real glory is being knocked to your knees and then coming back. That's real glory. That's the essence of it." – *Vince Lombardi*

"Baseball gives every American boy a chance to excel, not just to be as good as someone else, but to be better than someone else. This is the nature of man and the name of the game." – *Ted Williams*

"Baseball is a red-blooded sport for red-blooded men. It's no pink tea, and mollycoddles had better stay out. It's a struggle for supremacy, a survival of the fittest." – *Ty Cobb*

BASEBALL–LIFE STEP #7

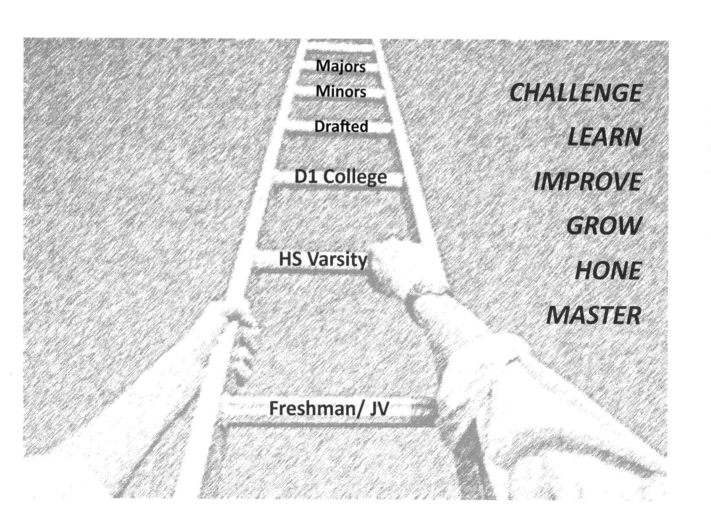

Majors
Minors
Drafted
D1 College
HS Varsity
Freshman/ JV

CHALLENGE
LEARN
IMPROVE
GROW
HONE
MASTER

BASEBALL-LIFE STEP #7

REACH FOR THE NEXT LEVEL

BARRIERS TO CHANGE:

Here are some of the main barriers to change which cause people to get stuck, resist growth, be incapable of making mental adjustments, and unable to Reach For The Next Level. Ask yourself if any of these barriers are holding you back from Reaching for the Next Level and fully embracing change and growth. *Check all that apply.*

- [ ] <u>Satisfaction with Status Quo</u> - It is easy to become satisfied with how things are. Why rock the boat or go through the trouble?

- [ ] <u>Lack of Motivation</u> - An absence of passion or drive, an inability to get worked up.

- [ ] <u>Fear of the unknown</u> - Comfortable with familiar routines. The unfamiliar makes me anxious, causing me to prefer what I know.

- [ ] <u>Lack of confidence</u> - I lack confidence and am not be sure I can handle the bigger game, greater pressure, higher expectations.

- [ ] <u>Low chance of success</u> - My expected reward is lower than my expected cost and effort, because I deem the chance of success and/or the value of success to be low.

- [ ] <u>Lack of Faith</u> - I don't believe that things will work out in the long run if I keep at it, and I cannot see the light at the end of the rainbow.

- [ ] <u>Fear of Failure</u> - I can't handle the possibility of failure, of being told I'm not good enough, am unwilling to try and fail, and look foolish in the process.

- [ ] <u>Ignorance</u> - I don't understand what I need to do or how to get the information.

- [ ] <u>Lack of Guidance</u> - I don't know who to turn to for guidance or support.

BASEBALL-LIFE STEP #7

REACH FOR THE NEXT LEVEL

You've learned to Operate Like a Champion and Lead Like a Champion. Step #7 is the first step in learning how to Grow Like a Champion. This Step is fundamentally about **change** and growth and learning to become comfortable with the uncomfortable. As you continue to play baseball, you will be continually subject to new challenges, and you must be ready to make adjustments. Step #7 prepares you to have the mindset to Reach For The Next Level, so you will not be surprised by this continuous process of growth required of you. When we are young, change is natural and effortless. But as we get older, we become more and more set in our ways. In fact, you could say that aging is the process of becoming more inflexible and less able to change. As a ball player, you must train yourself to stay flexible and adept at change and growth. Step #7 is a critical step in the process of being successful in baseball and in life. Baseball, like life, are intense funnels. In order to make it to the next step in the funnel, which weeds players quickly and ruthlessly, you must be prepared to grow, and grow quickly. While there are approximately 100,000 high school seniors playing baseball, there will only be 1/10 of these players playing at the college level. Are you willing to do what it takes to reach for the next level? For a while, you might be able to coast, perhaps getting by on natural athleticism or the "eye test", but at some point, you too are going to have to get used to not being the best, and learn how to fight for your position. Champions, the ones who succeed for the longest time, are those who have the drive to grow. Champions always want to improve and be the best at what they're doing. Champions don't allow themselves to rest on their laurels and past successes. As Babe Ruth said, "Yesterday's home runs don't win today's games." As uncomfortable as it is, you must learn to put yourself into new, more challenging situations, and be temporarily at the bottom of the pack, surrounded by players better than yourself, so that you quickly learn to make the adjustment, and work hard to catch up. Baseball, like life, is an endurance contest and the victory doesn't necessarily go to the fastest starter but to the man who finishes. Research points to the importance of grit and perseverance. Slow and steady wins the race. What do you need to do now to get better?

BASEBALL-LIFE STEP #7

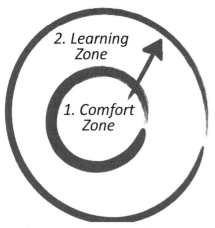

The key to Reaching For The Next Level is developing a habit of leaving your comfort zone and living in the LEARNING ZONE. First, you must have an awareness that there is a "next level." Then you must have an awareness of what that next level entails. Find the drive within yourself to play at that next level. Assume a beginner's mindset to learn and absorb everything you can about what it takes to make it at that next level. At each level, new things will be expected of you. While you may have been the best player on your little league team, it won't be the same in travel ball. You'll have to fight for your right to be in the starting lineup. In high school, unlike in travel ball where you are "paying" for the right to play, only the best players play. While you might practice 2-3 hours a day in high school, you'll be expected to practice 4-5 hours a day in college. At the pro level, the intensity is even greater. Each level will bring ever higher performance and commitment expectations.

- Begin to intentionally and deliberately prepare yourself for the next level of play.
- Play with players better than yourself.
- Be willing to put yourself in new situations that expose your weaknesses.
- Be willing to make mistakes, even fail for a while. Learn by doing. Learn by imitating.
- Pay attention to what works and what doesn't. Keep watching, learning, and adjusting.
- Be willing to fall to the bottom of the pack, and work yourself back to the top.
- Seek out the support and resources you need today to prepare yourself for tomorrow.
- Pay attention and observe how people do things and how people think at the higher level.
- Be curious. Ask lots of questions.
- Request feedback. Ask how you can get better.
- Improve your understanding, thinking, and analysis of the game.
- Hone your mental skills to deal with heightened competition and pressure.

BASEBALL-LIFE STEP #7

REACH FOR THE NEXT LEVEL

The habit of Reaching For The Next Level, and routinely forcing yourself to leave your comfort zone and live in the Learning Zone as a ball player sets you up well for future life success. One way this habit can serve you well is in managing your career. If you've learned how to continually grow and Reach For The Next Level, it ought to be relatively easy for you to extend this habit to the way you approach and manage your career.

What does it mean to reach for the next level in your career?
What is it that you are seeking? More money, status, contribution?
How will a learning mindset contribute to moving to the next level?

CAREER	REACH FOR THE NEXT LEVEL
Identify what it is you want from the next level	• You must know what it is you are seeking in that next level. • That next level must bring something more rewarding to make it worth it. • Is it more money, time, status, service, relationship?
Define your next challenge	• Be specific about what you want to take on next. • Be specific about how this next challenge will grow and develop you as a person.
Act the part	• If you want to be a sales manager, or division VP, figure out what you need to do before you've been promoted. Start acting the part now. • If you are credible and competent at doing things at the next level, people will see. • Acting the part means thinking, talking, dressing the part, signalling that you are indeed ready for that promotion.
Reinvent yourself for the times	• Stay ahead of the curve by anticipating how the trends are moving. • Don't allow yourself to be blindsided by changing times. • Reinvent yourself continually by maintaining a learner's mindset.

Practicing the art of Reaching For the Next Level, not only in baseball, but also in your career, will enable you to stay young, stimulated, challenged, fulfilled. Reaching For The Next Level makes you pro-active and energized for continual growth and success.

BASEBALL–LIFE STEP #7

REACH FOR THE NEXT LEVEL

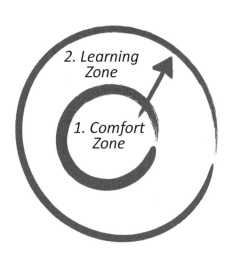

1. How will I know when I am ready and need to push away from my **Comfort Zone**?

_____

_____

_____

2. What are some ways I resist Reaching For the Next Level and moving into the **Learning Zone**?

_____

_____

_____

3. What will I do to move into my **Learning Zone**?

_____

_____

_____

4. What do I expect some of the challenges to be when I am in the **Learning Zone**?

_____

_____

_____

	AIM	**PREPARE**	**EXECUTE**
OPERATE LIKE A CHAMPION	**1** Set Positive Goals	**2** Train Intentionally	**3** Focus on the Process
LEAD LIKE A CHAMPION	**4** Identify Your Vision	**5** Live By Your Rules	**6** Write Your Own Story
GROW LIKE A CHAMPION	**7** Reach For The Next Level	**8** Grow Self-Awareness	**9** Raise Your Game

BASEBALL–LIFE STEP #8

GROW SELF-AWARENESS

Oh! I have thoughts:
- What am I thinking?
- What's my attitude?

Oh! I have feelings:
- What am I feeling?
- What's my mood?

Oh! Things going on in my body:
- How do I feel in my body?
- Am I calm or anxious?

- How am I behaving?
- What words am I using?
- Am I being thoughtful?
- Am I being a jerk?
- Am I getting distracted?
- Am I staying focused?
- Do I feel confident?
- Do I feel in control?
- Do I feel calm?
- Do I feel insecure?
- Am I afraid of failing?
- Do I give up too easily?
- Do I believe in myself?
- How committed am I?

BASEBALL-LIFE STEP #8

GROW SELF-AWARENESS

WHAT IS "SELF-AWARENESS"?

1) It is the capacity to see and observe yourself from a distance - what you think, say, and do.
2) It is a state of being continuously aware of yourself, both internally and externally.
3) Knowing your thoughts, feelings, motivations, strengths, weaknesses, qualities, what makes you happy, sad, angry, frustrated, and how you typically react in different situations.

WHAT DOES IT MEAN TO "GROW SELF-AWARENESS"?

1) Initially, it means to move from a state of unawareness of yourself as an "actor" or "agent."
2) Later, it means to be able to be more continuously aware of yourself and your state.
3) At mastery level, a heightened, continual awareness and understanding that regulates you.

WHAT ARE THE STEPS FOR "GROWING SELF-AWARENESS"?

1) First, recognizing that you can see yourself from a distance, like looking at an "object".
2) Second, checking in on yourself and observing yourself several times a day.
3) Third, maintaining a continual awareness of yourself and thoughts, words, language, actions, habits, discipline, mental toughness, behaviors, and choices.
4) Fourth, monitoring your thoughts, words, language, actions, habits, discipline, mental toughness, behaviors, choices in a way that aligns them to be how you want them to be.

WHY IS IT IMPORTANT TO "GROW SELF-AWARENESS"?

1) To cultivate the growing understanding that you have control over yourself.
2) To develop the self-discipline and self-determination that goes along with self-awareness.
3) To have real control over yourself and how your life goes.

WHAT HAPPENS IF YOU DON'T "GROW SELF-AWARENESS"?

1) You will not have the power to change the non-productive, non-helpful patterns of your life.
2) You will not understand or believe you can fully control yourself and your life.
3) You will not be able to achieve true mastery of your craft, whether it is baseball or life.

"I've always had a certain self-awareness about my abilities. Many baseball players are blind to their own weaknesses. I, however, was always keenly aware of mine, and I sought to improve them on a daily basis." – *Bo Durkac*

"Your visions will become clear only when you can look into your own heart. Who looks outside, dreams. Who looks inside, awakens." – *C.G. Jung*

"You can't get away from yourself by moving from one place to another." – *Earnest Hemingway*

"Losers never know why they are losing. They will mention injuries, officiating, the weather, and bad breaks." – *George Allen*

"The only person who can pull me down is myself, and I'm not going to let myself pull me down anymore." – *C.J.C.*

"Listen to yourself. Catch yourself. Change your thoughts, and yourself." – *Harvey Dorfman*

"Difficulties in life are intended to make us better, not bitter." – *Dan Reeves*

"The battles that count aren't the ones for gold medals. The struggles within yourself – the invisible battles inside all of us – that's where it's at." – *Jesse Owens*

BASEBALL-LIFE STEP #8

GROW SELF-AWARENESS

After you have learned how to Reach For The Next Level, the next Step to Growing Like a Champion is to Grow Self-Awareness. Step #8 is critical to Growing Like a Champion because without Self-Awareness, you will not be able to recognize or change what's not working, in your mind, heart, and habits. Champions develop the capacity to observe and know themselves, especially what works and what doesn't. By developing your self-awareness, you will understand your strengths, weaknesses, challenges, how you lack discipline, lack focus, aren't paying appropriate attention, what to improve. Your growing self-awareness will tell you if you are mentally tough or easily intimidated or distracted. Your growing self-awareness will help you identify things that you aren't doing well: Are you afraid of asking questions? Are you afraid to ask for help? Are you afraid of feedback? Are you too cocky? Are you bad at taking suggestions? Do you lack confidence? Are you selfish? If you don't master Step #8, it will be impossible to be successful in Step #9, Raise Your Game, because you won't have the awareness, understanding, or self-control to do so. While Step #7 asked us to learn to be comfortable with the uncomfortable, Step #8 asks us to learn to pay attention to things we typically take for granted and ignore. Typically, our focus is on things outside ourselves: where the ball is hit, what the coach said, what my friends did. Step #8, however, challenges you to re-direct your focus to things inside yourself. Each Step, from Steps #1-9, asks you to do something that initially feels quite difficult, but over time becomes truly satisfying. You will find that Growing Your Self-Awareness to a point of mastery will feel truly satisfying, because you will gain the self-control to be the kind of person you truly want to be, thoughtful, respected, calm, relaxed, high performing, effective, motivated, kind, a team player, someone who says the right things, and does the right things, and is a real leader and asset for your organization. Step #8 paves the way to Raising your Game. It is a necessary step to real growth and maturation. Champions are intensely self-absorbed, in the best way. They pay attention to themselves, understand themselves, nurture themselves, know how to unlock their own potential, and get the best out of themselves.

BASEBALL–LIFE STEP #8

GROW SELF–AWARENESS   FUNDAMENTALS

Every improvement begins with self-awareness. Become aware of the fact that you can pay attention to your internal experience and your outer behaviors. Observe yourself as you would observe someone you want to know well.

A. Develop awareness of YOU.

PRACTICE: Every day at the beginning of baseball practice, ask yourself 3 questions: How's my energy? What's my mood? What is my body language saying? Take 3 minutes to answer each question with at least 3 descriptive sentences. Rate your internal experience as RED, YELLOW, or GREEN.

B. Track your behavior and pay attention to your actions and words.

PRACTICE: Every night, right before you go to sleep, think back to three interactions you had with people during the day. Reflect on your behavior. Were you friendly? respectful? funny? Did you put someone down? Did you try to intimidate somebody? Were you rude? Rate your behavior as RED, YELLOW, or GREEN.

RED: Things are bad. Something is off. STOP.

C. Observe your routines and habits.

PRACTICE: Every day, when you are waking up, review what you are going to do today, and ask yourself how this fits into your habitual pattern. Who do you rely on most each day? Who do you spend the most time talking to? Who helps you with homework? Do you do speed, strength, flexibility conditioning outside of practice? How much time do you spend texting, watching TV, and on the internet? Rate your habits as RED, YELLOW, or GREEN.

YELLOW: Things are tense/not great. CAUTION.

GREEN: Things are fine. KEEP GOING.

BASEBALL-LIFE STEP #8

GROW SELF-AWARENESS

☐ Coachable	☐ Adjusts quickly	☐ Difficulty taking direction
☐ Know what I want	☐ Attentive	☐ Unmotivated
☐ Good Attitude	☐ Not Defensive	☐ Get Discouraged Quickly
☐ Focused	☐ Inquisitive	☐ Unfocused
☐ Hard Working	☐ Makes Eye Contact	☐ Complain a lot
☐ Confident	☐ Tries New Things	☐ Selfish
☐ A Leader	☐ Optimistic	☐ Lack Confidence
☐ Continual Learner	☐ Mature	☐ Easily Bored
☐ Growth Mindset	☐ Listens Well	☐ Stubborn
☐ Disciplined	☐ Fast Learner	☐ Disorderly
☐ Ask for Feedback	☐ Grateful	☐ Hate to be criticized

☑ *Check all the intangible qualities you possess or are working on that help you be a better player.*

☒ *Put an X for all the qualities you display that hurt your prospects of being a better player.*

BASEBALL—LIFE STEP #8

GROW SELF—AWARENESS

The habit of Growing Self-Awareness, and developing a habit of checking in on yourself, your thoughts, feelings, actions, mood, attitude, mindset, confidence level, and degree of calmness as a ball player sets you up well for life success. One way this habit can serve you well is in your relationship with a significant other. If you've learned how to be self-aware on an almost continuous basis, regulating and monitoring yourself as a matter of habit, it ought to be relatively easy for you to extend this habit to a relationship with a special other.

What does self-awareness bring to a relationship?
How can you bring awareness to the relationship itself?
How does self-awareness help you to have a stronger relationship?

RELATIONSHIP	SELF-AWARENESS
Understand yourself	• If you understand yourself, you can communicate your needs and wants effectively. • When you understand yourself, you know what you are looking for in someone else.
Know your triggers	• This helps you to avoid getting into an unpleasant situation. • This helps you avoid reacting to your triggers, knowing ahead of time it will be hard.
Be aware of mood	• This helps you give the other person a heads up when you are in a bad mood. • This helps you to avoid big decisions when you are not in the right frame of mind.
Keep your boundaries	• This helps you to avoid feeling bossed around or controlled by someone else. • This helps you to avoid being disrespected, unappreciated, or abused.

Practicing the art of Growing Self-Awareness, not only in baseball, but also in your relationship with your significant other, will enable you to have a strong, nurturing, fulfilling, successful relationships with a special someone. Growing Your Self-Awareness means that you are so in tune with yourself that you can communicate effectively what you need and want, what works for you and what doesn't, what upsets you and what makes you happy.

BASEBALL-LIFE STEP #8

GROW SELF-AWARENESS

YOU HAVE MASTERED STEP #8 IF...

1. You are aware when you are having a good day.

2. You are aware when you are having a bad day.

3. You know what you need to do to avoid bad situations.

4. You know how to self-correct from a bad moment.

5. You know how to bring yourself back to center.

6. You know how to avoid being triggered, because you know your triggers and you know your responses, and how to avoid stepping into traps.

7. You know, appreciate, and leverage your strengths; You know your weaknesses, and have developed strategies to compensate for them.

BASEBALL–LIFE STEP #8

GROW SELF–AWARENESS

One of the most helpful things we can do as parents is become more aware of our impact on our son and ball player. By growing our own self-awareness, and becoming more sensitive of our impact on them and others, we can begin to adjust our behaviors and words to be more appropriate. For example, are you aware of the impact when you *don't* go to your son's games? Are you aware of the impact when you *do* go to his games? How does your being in the stands affect his mood and playing? What's the impact when you pepper him with lots of advice before a game? What is the impact when you are in a sour mood after a tough game where things didn't go his way, he struck out on bases loaded, or let lots of runs in with his pitching? What is your impact when you say "Good job. I really liked the way you kept your composure."? Here is a checklist to help parents grow their own self-awareness and become more sensitive, supportive, and helpful to their ball players.

Mark the circle that is most like you

	Not at all	Barely	Sometimes	Frequently	Always
1. I am very competitive by nature and hate it when my son does poorly.	○	○	○	○	○
2. When the umpire makes a bad call, I'll make a comment from the stands.	○	○	○	○	○
3. I know when my son is feeling bad about himself, and try to lift him up.	○	○	○	○	○
4. When I am feeling anxious, I will move myself away from others.	○	○	○	○	○
5. My son can tell when I'm upset with him, even if I don't say anything.	○	○	○	○	○
6. I'm too busy, and don't have time to go to any of his games.	○	○	○	○	○
7. I make my son nervous when I go to his games.	○	○	○	○	○
8. I am proud of my son, and I tell him so in lots of ways.	○	○	○	○	○

BASEBALL–LIFE STEP #8

GROW SELF–AWARENESS

As a coach, you are a teacher, motivator, strategist, and leader. As a coach, your attunement to each player's temperament and situation, and your attunement to the team's chemistry can develop as you become more self-aware of your impact on others, and how your words and actions affect how the team performs. The savviest coaches are acutely aware of the impact that they have, and they know exactly how to get the best out of each and every one of their players. They know each player's strengths and weaknesses, both physically and mentally. They can see raw talent and potential, they have a growth mindset, and know that their team is only as strong as their weakest player. They know what to do with their most talented players. But they also know how to nurture and bring out the best in their weaker players. They know that some players need to be pushed a bit harder, while other players need more of a soft touch. They know that some players are more mature and can take feedback, while other players are more sensitive. They know which players have all the confidence in the world, and which players need more encouragement.

Mark the circle that is most like you

	Not at all	Barely	Sometimes	Frequently	Always
1. I have no tolerance for assistants and players who question me.	◯	◯	◯	◯	◯
2. I have little patience for players that don't follow my rules.	◯	◯	◯	◯	◯
3. When a player makes a bad play, I immediately yell at them about it.	◯	◯	◯	◯	◯
4. I get disappointed and angry when my players don't make easy plays.	◯	◯	◯	◯	◯
5. I allow my players to make mistakes and grow.	◯	◯	◯	◯	◯
6. I believe my players have capacity to grow with clear, positive instruction.	◯	◯	◯	◯	◯
7. I take a long term view to developing my players.	◯	◯	◯	◯	◯
8. I am really clear what I expect from each player and the team as a whole.	◯	◯	◯	◯	◯
9. I explain my thinking and strategy so everyone is on the same page.	◯	◯	◯	◯	◯

BASEBALL-LIFE STEP #8

GROW SELF-AWARENESS   SELF-ASSESSMENT

Now that you've begun to develop a habit of paying attention to your own thoughts and feelings, as well as your behaviors and words, you are ready to become more self-aware of yourself with baseball. Circle the appropriate responses.

Step #1: How well do I Set Positive Goals for myself in baseball? (Excellent | Well | OK | Poorly)

Step #2: How well do I Train Intentionally? (Excellent | Well | OK | Poorly)

Step #3: How well do I Focus On The Process? (Excellent | Well | OK | Poorly)

Part 1: How well am I Operating Like a Champion? (Excellent | Well | OK | Poorly)

Step #4: How well have I Identified My Vision with Baseball? (Excellent | Well | OK | Poorly)

Step #5: How well do I Live By My Rules? (Excellent | Well | OK | Poorly)

Step #6: How well am I Writing My Own Story? (Excellent | Well | OK | Poorly)

Part 2: How well am I Leading Like a Champion? (Excellent | Well | OK | Poorly)

Step #7: How well am I Reaching For The Next Level in Baseball? (Excellent | Well | OK | Poorly)

Step #8: How well am I Growing My Self-Awareness? (Excellent | Well | OK | Poorly)

Step #9: How well am I Raising My Game? (Excellent | Well | OK | Poorly)

Part 3: How well am I Growing Like a Champion? (Excellent | Well | OK | Poorly)

• My 3 greatest strengths as a player are: A)_____, B)_____, C)_____

• The 3 things I most need to work on in baseball are: A)_____, B)_____, C)_____

• The 3 distractions that cause me to lose my focus quickest are: A)_____, B)_____, C)_____

• In the last game I played, my confidence was (High | Medium | Low). Explain: _____

• I play better when A) People believe in me, B) I'm proving skeptics wrong, C) I am relaxed

• My baseball IQ and knowledge of baseball, past & present, is: Excellent | Good | Fair | Poor.

	AIM	**PREPARE**	**EXECUTE**
OPERATE LIKE A CHAMPION	**1** Set Positive Goals	**2** Train Intentionally	**3** Focus on the Process
LEAD LIKE A CHAMPION	**4** Identify Your Vision	**5** Live By Your Rules	**6** Write Your Own Story
GROW LIKE A CHAMPION	**7** Reach For The Next Level	**8** Grow Self-Awareness	**9** Raise Your Game

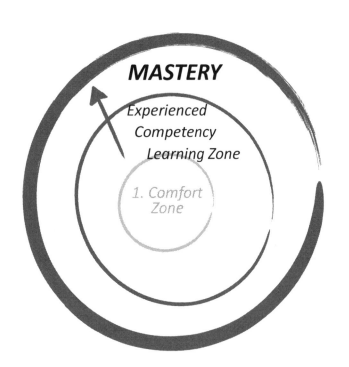

MASTERY

Experienced
Competency
Learning Zone

1. Comfort Zone

Step #9 is the culminating Step of the 9-Step Blueprint for Baseball and Life Success. It is about Raising Your Game to the level of **Mastery**. All the preceding Steps have been building us to this point. What we are striving for as baseball players and as human beings is to be at the top of our game, with a deep command of our skill and knowledge. To do this takes years of practice, setbacks, intentionality, training, and perseverance. What makes **Mastery** so rare, so dear, so sweet, and so valuable, is that you cannot *buy* Mastery. The only way to attain **Mastery** is by determination, hard work, and some talent and good luck.

"Each honest calling, each walk of life, has its own elite, its own aristocracy based on excellence of performance." – James Conant

BASEBALL–LIFE STEP #9

WHAT DOES IT MEAN TO "RAISE YOUR GAME"?
1) It means to move from the Learning Zone to Mastery.
2) It means to not be satisfied with merely competent or OK.
3) It means to push for the highest possible level of human performance.

WHAT IS REQUIRED TO "RAISE YOUR GAME"?
1) The first requirement is competency of the fundamentals of the game, which requires operational excellence, as described in Steps #1,2,3.
2) The second requirement is clear direction for your journey, which requires personal leadership excellence, as described in Steps #4,5,6.
3) The third requirement is an intentional process of learning, growth, and development, as described in Steps #7,8,9.

WHAT ARE THE STEPS TO "RAISING YOUR GAME" AND MASTERY?
1) In the Learning Zone, we are learners and ***Novices***.
2) Then we become ***Competent*** at the Intermediate level, able to perform with a degree of concentration and effort.
3) Next we become ***Experienced*** at this new level.
4) Last, a few attain ***Mastery*** at this new level.

WHY IS IT MEANINGFUL TO "RAISE YOUR GAME" and AIM FOR MASTERY?
1) Mastery is something we should all aim for, but not everyone will attain Mastery. Mastery is a path, not a destination. We become masterly, we don't *possess* mastery.
2) You cannot pay to be masterful, it can only come from within. It is ultimately about a way of cultivating oneself, an orientation towards mastery that becomes a way of life.
3) That's why those who Raise their Game to the Mastery Level are rewarded so handsomely.

"In baseball, you don't know nothing." *– Yogi Berra*	"It's what you learn after you know it all that counts." *– John Wooden*

"If people knew how hard I worked to get my mastery, it wouldn't seem so wonderful at all." *– Michelangelo*

"He who stops being better stops being good." *– Oliver Cromwell*

"I don't think much of a man who is not wiser today than he was yesterday." *– Abraham Lincoln*	"Who dares to teach must never cease to learn." *– John Dana*
"Only one who devotes himself to a cause with his whole strength and soul can be a true master. For this reason mastery demands all of a person." *– Albert Einstein*	"It's unbelievable how much you don't know about the game you've been playing all your life." *– Mickey Mantle*

"It is time to reverse this prejudice against conscious effort and to see the powers we gain through practice and discipline as eminently inspring and even miraculous." *– Robert Greene*

BASEBALL–LIFE STEP #9

0%   100%
degree of control

GRIT

This is determined by your
determination, resilience, and
willingness to follow Steps #1-#9.
Do you have 100% GRIT?

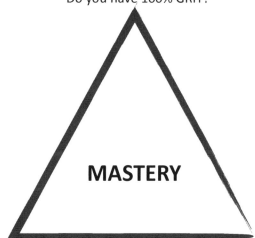

MASTERY

50%

0%   100%
degree of control

LUCK

We partly make
our luck and partly
enjoy our luck.

0%   100%
degree of control

TALENT

Our talent is somewhat
pre-determined,
though we can improve
on our raw materials.

The Mastery Triangle illustrates the 3 main ingredients for Raising Your Game to Mastery Level.
The one ingredient you have full control over is your GRIT to follow Steps #1-9.

BASEBALL–LIFE STEP #9

PART 1

SETTING POSITIVE GOALS

- [ ] Identify 2-4 Positive Goals
- [ ] Outline 3 Action steps / Goal
- [ ] Do the 3 Action steps

TRAINING INTENTIONALLY

- [ ] Hone your Fundamentals
- [ ] Hone your Mental Skills
- [ ] Hone your Muscle Memory
- [ ] Control your Attitude
- [ ] Establish a clear routine

FOCUS ON THE PROCESS

- [ ] Customize Your Process
- [ ] Master Focusing
- [ ] Master Relaxing
- [ ] Master Locking In
- [ ] Master Execution

PART 2

IDENTIFY YOUR VISION

- [ ] Write your 10 yr vision
- [ ] Write your 25 yr vision
- [ ] Identify stepping stones

FOLLOW YOUR RULES

- [ ] Set your Mindset Rules
- [ ] Set your Habit Rules
- [ ] Set your Language Rules
- [ ] Set your Conduct Rules
- [ ] Be Accountable to your Rules

WRITE YOUR OWN STORY

- [ ] Identify your major events
- [ ] Identify your story outcomes
- [ ] Identify actions to take
- [ ] Write a story linking elements
- [ ] Tell your story to others

PART 3

REACH FOR NEXT LEVEL

- [ ] Acknowledge Comfort Zone
- [ ] Move to Learning Zone
- [ ] Assume Beginner's mind

GROW SELF-AWARENESS

- [ ] Do Intangibles Checklist
- [ ] Track your energy and mood
- [ ] Track your actions and words
- [ ] Observe own routines/habits
- [ ] Do Self-Assessment

RAISE YOUR GAME

- [ ] Determine your GRIT %
- [ ] Take Action to improve each Step to "Excellent" rating
- [ ] Make Adjustments in each Step to improve your efforts
- [ ] Be accountable for *Excellent*

BASEBALL–LIFE STEP #9

The habit of Raising Your Game and developing mastery as a ball player sets you up well for life success. Developing Mastery takes a disciplined approach to baseball and life, requiring all 9 Steps from Setting Goals, Intentional Action, Focusing without distractions, to having Vision, Rules, Purpose, to Learning, Self-Awareness, and Raising Competency. If you've learned the process of developing mastery in baseball, it ought to be straightforward for you to extend this habit to whatever else you choose to excel at.

How are Mastery and Self-Mastery related?
How does Operating, Leading, Growing Like a Champion lead to Self-Mastery?
Do you want to be masterful in all areas of your life?

LIFE AREAS	MASTERY
Career	• Raising Your Game to Self-Mastery will help you to be successful in your career • Being masterful means having valuable skills, competencies, and insight.
Relationship	• Raising Your Game to Self-Mastery will help you to be successful in your relationships. • Being masterful means having clear boundaries, being thoughtful, and collaborative.
Money	• Raising Your Game to Self-Mastery will help you to be successful with money. • Being masterful means understanding, managing, and investing money well.
Health	• Raising Your Game to Self-Mastery will help you to be successful in self-care. • Being masterful means taking care of your emotional, mental, and physical health.

Practicing the art of Raising Your Game, not only in baseball, but in all realms of your life, will enable you to have a deep sense of competency, fulfillment, and joy. Raising Your Game means having an orientation towards doing the best that you can do in all realms of your life, and being purposeful, intentional, and deliberate in how you approach life and relationships.

There are 3 areas where you, as a coach, can Raise Your Game and the team's performance:

1. Team Chemistry

Championships are won by teams not individuals. All great teams win by the combination of talents and skills of the players on the team. While some team might, on the surface, seem more physically gifted and talented, another team that is less physically gifted, but has stronger team chemistry may end up doing better. Team chemistry helps a team turn double plays more easily, be more connected to one another, be more positive and play more selflessly. Team chemistry, team confidence, and team spirit are all critical ingredients that the best coaches intentionally foster. Boys have a natural desire to belong and contribute to a team, and are naturally prone to be loyal to their own team. How can a coach enhance these natural inclinations and bring out the team's best? Having a sensitivity to the existing team dynamics is helpful. Who is considered a leader by the boys themselves? Which boys enhance the team's comraderie, follow orders well, and are excellent team players? Which boys are most admired by the others? Which boys can be counted on to be responsible and make good decisions? How do you cultivate the right amount of healthy competitive tension that is productive but does not pit one player against another and undermine team cohesion? Improving team chemistry and comraderie will Raise Your Game.

2. Personal Self-Mastery

The second way you can raise your game is by doing a regular self-assessment, and working to improve in the areas that you are weakest. For example, are you organized? Do you run efficient practices where players get the most out of their time and don't get overly tired? Are you perceived as fair and honest? Do you keep your word and do what you say you'll do? Do your players and parents trust you? Do you try to develop all your players? Do you play favorites? Are you firm but loving? Are you clear about your expectations and rules? Are you able to cultivate the support and loyalty of your boosters? The greater your personal character and integrity, the higher your stock goes, and the more you Raise Your Game.

3. Statistics and Strategy

The last area is the most technical and there are whole books about it. Baseball is famous for having lots of data and has been revolutionized at the Major League level by data analysis, otherwise called sabermetrics. Some of the lessons can and should be filtered down to the lower levels, where the insights can have a profound impact on the level of a team's play. Here are just a few:

A. ***On-Base-Percentage***: Pay attention not just to a batter's Batting Average (BA), but also to their OBP, because this often paints a different, more nuanced story about their contribution to runs production, wins, hitting tendencies, and ability. "OBP is the most important variable - more important than SLG or AVG. Given any group of 9 hitters, the batting order that scores the most runs is the one ranked in descending order of OBP." *Baseball Between The Numbers*, 2007, p.39.

B. ***Quality At Bats***: A batter who raises the pitch count by 7-11 pitches for a given at bat is valuable, even if he doesn't get a hit, because it raises the pitch count and gives the team a shot at the next best pitcher.

C. ***Well-Hit Ball Metric***: Pay attention to the number of well-hit balls, not just batting average. 0/5 isn't poor hitting if he's making good contact.

D. ***Hitter Ability and Batting Order***: The best hitters should be hitting #1, #2, and #4 in the lineup, while the 4th and 5th best should be in the #3 and #5 slots.

E. ***Base Stealing***: It makes more sense to steal when a game is tied or you're ahead, but a bad idea to steal when you are behind, as the cost of an out is higher because it prevents a big scoring inning.

F. ***The effect of a base stealing attempt on the batter***: An attempted base steal reduces the batter's wOBA significantly, compared to a situation if the runner stays put, because it disturbs the batter's concentration.

G. ***Small Ball, Sacrifice Bunts and Hits***: A sacrifice bunt attempt early in the game in a low run-scoring game is okay with no outs, but letting better batters swing away will generate more runs.

H. ***Throwing First Pitch Strikes and Game Theory***: Pitchers shouldn't throw the same pitch in any specific situation so that the batter cannot guess what's coming.

I. ***The Truth about "Hot streaks" and "Slumps"***: Hot streaks and slumps are perceived by humans, but are not true statistically. To assess a player's ability, you need 40 or 50 at bats, or 2 season's worth, not just 3 or 4 or 10 of his latest at bats!

BASEBALL–LIFE STEP #9

RAISE YOUR GAME

As you become more serious about being a baseball player, you need to educate yourself about baseball history, so that you can share a common language with other baseball lovers. Now that you're a student of the game, it is important to expand your knowledge and awareness of baseball, America's game. Who were Tinkers, Evers & Chance? What was the the 1919 Black Sox scandal? Who were Ruth & Gherig? What was their importance to baseball and our country's history of the 1920's? Did Doubleday or Cartwright invent America's game of baseball? Who was Branch Rickie? Hank Aaron? Jackie Robinson? What was the "Shot Heard Around the World"? Who were "Willie, Mickey & the Duke"? Why the DH? Who were the cheaters in baseball? Can you name them and what they did? How has the history of baseball paralleled that of American history? And finally, who is your favorite player, your favorite team and why? Does your favorite player do what you do now or what you eventually want to do? Educate yourself about Baseball. It will deepen your appreciation of the game you are playing.

Throughout the ages, baseball players have been nicknamed. See if you can identify some!

The Georgia Peach	Wizard	The Iron Horse	Dr. Strange Glove
The Big Train	Spaceman	The Bambino	The Bird
The Sultan of Swat	Human Rain Delay	The Rajah	Mr. Baseball
The Meal Ticket	The Penguin	The Lip	Vacuum Cleaner
Yankee Clipper	The Big Cat	The Thumper	Mad Hungarian
The Kid	The Big Unit	The Man	Reading Rifle
Mr. Cub	Mr. November	Hammering Hank	The Bulldog
Splendid Splinter	The Flying Dutchman	Flatbush Fox	Big Papa

BASEBALL-LIFE STEP #9

YOU HAVE MASTERED STEP #9 IF...

1. You are goal-focused, disicplined, and present in every moment.

2. You have a clear sense of who you are, what you stand for, where you are headed.

3. You have a deep sense of integrity and personal rules and values.

4. You have a learning mindset where you have a thirst to learn and grow.

5. You have a deep understanding of baseball history and baseball statistics.

6. You have a heightened self-awareness that helps you to be more calm and controlled.

7. You are admired and emulated as a role model by others, and find yourself increasingly being a teacher to those who desire to become masterful themselves.

Babe Ruth

Willy Mays

Hank Aaron

Baseball Masters

BASEBALL-LIFE STEP #9

RAISE YOUR GAME

GET TO THE NEXT LEVEL

REACH FOR THE NEXT LEVEL

GROWTH & CHANGE

GROW YOUR AWARENESS

You, only you, are in charge of how much you learn and grow. Even in school, no one can really force you to study and learn if you refuse to do so. All that teachers and coaches can do is show you the way. It's up to you as a student and athlete to decide how much you are going to take in. *"You can lead a horse to water, but you can't make it drink."* The ball is totally in your court. How much dedication and commitment will you devote to your personal growth on and off the field? At the end of the day, it's all about growth. Why do we devote our final 3 Steps to How to Grow Like A Champion? Because growth towards mastery is the culmination of all the hard work, intentional training, competitions and performances. Because growth towards mastery has its own intrinsic meaningfulness. Masters embody the spirit of continual learning. Why? They've reached what others would consider the top, the peak, the pinnacle. So what motivates them to keep striving, learning, changing, growing? Why can't they just rest and stop? Because they know, more than anyone else, that the fun is not in the destination (being at the "top"). Rather the fun is precisely, precisely in the journey! Having attained Mastery, there is nothing better than challenging yourself to the next mountain top, just because you can. Once you achieve Mastery, your work is not done. Your work has just begun.

RAISE YOUR GAME

BASEBALL-LIFE STEP #9

RAISE YOUR GAME

In this book, we've outlined a 9-Step Blueprint for Success in Baseball and Life. We wanted to produce an easy-to-understand book that laid out, in straightforward fashion, a clear blueprint for your success. We wrote the book we wish we had ourselves growing up. You may find it surprising that a blueprint for baseball success could so seamlessly translate to school, friendship, career, relationship, and money. We hope it motivates you to follow the 9-Step Blueprint. But we also want to be realistic. What's difficult isn't understanding the blueprint. What's difficult is implementing the blueprint, actually *building* the house. There are a lot of "success blueprints" out there. What you have to do is believe in the blueprint, and *stick with the program*.

As human beings, we can find it easy to deviate from the plan for various reasons. We can get lazy, tired, depressed, lose confidence, be hurt by naysayers and haters, sabotage ourselves. Part of us knows we're hurting ourselves, but sometimes we can't muster the inner strength to self-correct, and get back on the right path. It's easier to go with what's easy in the moment rather than stick with a plan for the long run. When everyone else seems to be having fun, why should we make ourselves miserable? That's often how self-discipline can feel – too difficult to sustain.

Though this 9-Step Blueprint is straightforward, we can't promise that it's necessarily *easy*. But easy isn't what Champions are after. Champions are driven by Challenge and Excellence, not the easy road. Champions come to know the inherent meaningfulness of living a life of discipline, intention, and grit that moves them step by step towards mastery. Each time you find yourself at a new level of play, you'll want to re-visit these 9 Steps again. These 9 Steps are meant to be continuously repeated, over and over again, through your whole baseball career and life. Because it's a formula for continued success and mastery, a formula to continue Raising Your Game, not just for today, but for your whole life.

> It's fun. Baseball's fun.

> – Yogi Berra

BASEBALL–LIFE PARALLELS

BASEBALL	LIFE

As you read the book, fill in some Baseball-Life parallels you've discovered over time;
the ways in which some baseball lesson applies to life, or some life lesson applies to baseball.

BASEBALL–LIFE NOTES

Made in the USA
Middletown, DE
16 January 2022